E-Research in Educational Contexts

T0362192

This book explores the impact of e-research in education and the opportunities presented by a new generation of research approaches and tools. 'E-research' is an umbrella term that encompasses all digital research methods used for data collection and analysis including those involving handheld mobile devices. This is a current concern as the emergence of online tools that enable people to collaborate, create, and share information has led to the widespread use of these new digital research methods. Indeed, new tools and technologies are emerging almost daily and are being taken up by researchers for their ease of data collection and analysis.

As a result the book investigates the implications of how we conceptualise educational research in the digital age. In addressing a range of key themes, from the ethics of e-research to the relationships between researchers and participants, the book presents original studies from a variety of educational contexts where digital tools are being used. It will be of value to postgraduate students in the social sciences, academic researchers, and policy makers.

This book was originally published as a special issue of the *International Journal of Research & Method in Education.*

Jocelyn Wishart is a Senior Lecturer in Education at the University of Bristol, UK. She specialises in researching the use of new and emerging technologies to support teaching and learning. She is Membership Secretary for the International Association for Mobile Learning and is currently working on a book tentatively entitled *Mobile Learning in Schools.* Prior to entering teacher education she taught science, psychology, and ICT in secondary schools.

Michael Thomas is an Associate Professor in Digital Education and Learning at the University of Central Lancashire, UK. He has taught at universities in Germany and Japan, and is the author or editor of fifteen books, mostly in the field of technology-enhanced learning. He is lead editor of the book series *Digital Education and Learning* and *Advances in Digital Language Learning and Teaching.*

E-Research in Educational Contexts

The Roles of Technologies, Ethics and Social Media

Edited by
Jocelyn Wishart and Michael Thomas

LONDON AND NEW YORK

First published 2017
by Routledge

2 Park Square, Milton Park, Abingdon, Oxfordshire OX14 4RN
52 Vanderbilt Avenue, New York, NY 10017

Routledge is an imprint of the Taylor & Francis Group, an informa business

First issued in paperback 2018

Introduction, Chapters 1, 3–6 © 2017 Taylor & Francis
Chapter 2 © Sarah Parsons, Karen Guldberg, Kaśka Porayska-Pomsta and
Rachael Lee

British Library Cataloguing in Publication Data
A catalogue record for this book is available from the British Library

ISBN 13: 978-1-138-22962-4 (hbk)
ISBN 13: 978-0-367-07577-4 (pbk)

Typeset in Times New Roman
by RefineCatch Limited, Bungay, Suffolk

Publisher's Note
The publisher accepts responsibility for any inconsistencies that may have
arisen during the conversion of this book from journal articles to book chapters,
namely the possible inclusion of journal terminology.

Disclaimer
Every effort has been made to contact copyright holders for their permission to
reprint material in this book. The publishers would be grateful to hear from any
copyright holder who is not here acknowledged and will undertake to rectify
any errors or omissions in future editions of this book.

Contents

Contents

Citation Information

The chapters in this book were originally published in the *International Journal of Research & Method in Education*, volume 38, issue 3 (August 2015). When citing this material, please use the original page numbering for each article, as follows:

Chapter 5

Hermeneutics as a methodological resource for understanding empathy in on-line learning environments
Margaret Walshaw and Wayne Duncan
International Journal of Research & Method in Education, volume 38, issue 3 (August 2015), pp. 304–319

Chapter 6

Advancing ethics frameworks and scenario-based learning to support educational research into mobile learning
Trish Andrews, Laurel Evelyn Dyson and Jocelyn Wishart
International Journal of Research & Method in Education, volume 38, issue 3 (August 2015), pp. 320–334

For any permission-related enquiries please visit:
http://www.tandfonline.com/page/help/permissions

Notes on Contributors

Trish Andrews is a Senior Lecturer in Higher Education with the Teaching and Educational Development Institute at the University of Queensland, Brisbane, Australia.

Daniel Chazan is a Professor in the Department of Teaching and Learning, Policy and Leadership at the University of Maryland, USA.

Wayne Duncan is based at Northern Southland College, Queenstown, New Zealand.

Laurel Evelyn Dyson is a Lecturer in Information Technology at the University of Technology, Sydney, Australia.

Jonathan Earley is an IT Manager and Web Developer at the National Centre for Research Methods, Southampton, UK.

Karen Guldberg is currently Director of the Autism Centre for Education and Research in the School of Education at the University of Birmingham, UK.

Patricio Herbst is Professor of Education and Mathematics, and Chair of the Educational Studies Program at the University of Michigan, Ann Arbor, MI, USA.

Daniel Kilburn is a Tutor in Geography and the Built Environment in the UCL Centre for Languages and International Education, UCL, UK.

Rachael Lee is based at the Sussex Community NHS Trust, Speech and Language Therapy Service, Lancing, UK.

Sarah Parsons is a Reader and Head of the Social Justice and Inclusive Education Research Centre at the University of Southampton, UK.

Kaśka Porayska-Pomsta is a Reader in Adaptive Technologies for Learning and an RCUK Academic Fellow at the London Knowledge Lab, Institute of Education, UK.

Michael Thomas is an Associate Professor in Digital Education and Learning at the University of Central Lancashire, UK.

Sylvi Vigmo is a Senior Lecturer and Researcher in the Department of Education, Communication and Learning at Gothenburg University, Sweden.

Margaret Walshaw is a Professor in the Institute of Education at Massey University, Palmerston North, New Zealand.

Marina Wernholm is a doctoral student in the Department of Pedagogy at Linnæus University, Sweden.

Jocelyn Wishart is a Senior Lecturer in Education at the University of Bristol, UK.

INTRODUCTION

Introducing e-research in educational contexts, digital methods and issues arising

The emergence of Web 2.0 tools that enable people to collaborate, create and share information online has led to the use of new digital research methods. Across a range of contexts in education, these new practices are changing the landscape of research collaboration, data collection, analysis and dissemination and addressing the impact of these e-research tools in education has become a topical concern. Following the *British Journal of Educational Technology* (Markauskaite and Reimann 2014), this is the second special issue of a peer-reviewed journal addressing e-research in educational contexts and the surrounding issues and concerns from a UK-based journal in less than 12 months. Educational researchers now have to grapple with the challenges presented by, as Greenhow, Robelia and Hughes (2009) so succinctly put, an expanding research tool kit and emerging ethical issues arising from its use. In their editorial from the earlier special issue, Markauskaite and Reimann (2014) point out that this expansion of research tools means not only employing new research instruments and techniques but also exploring new ways to do research and, indeed, new ways to be a researcher. Whether employing online and digital tools such as social media, virtual reality, mobile apps and digital games in educational research has directly led to the emergence of new ethical challenges, as implied above by Greenhow, Robelia, and Hughes (2009), is arguable. Nevertheless, the presence of both is covered in this special issue of the *International Journal of Research & Method in Education* in which we are also concerned with the ways that digital innovations are changing how we think about research, how research is conducted and implications of this for how we conceptualize education.

Our interest in the impact and opportunities underlying e-research in education stems from a one-day symposium held in May 2013 and funded by Digital Social Research, a phase of the Economic and Social Research Council (ESRC)'s e-Social Science programme set up between 2010 and 2012 for established and new researchers to discuss the use of new digital research methods and their associated methodological impact. The symposium itself aimed to address key issues related to the Digital Social Research Strategy, particularly in relation to the challenges posed by data collection and analysis in the digital age, including trust and quality, interoperability and data preservation in educational contexts.

Aims of the ESRC's e-Social Science programme (ESRC 2012) were to maximize the uptake, use and impact of new digital technologies across the social science community. While the e-Social Science programme of work was focused upon building digital tools and technologies to support new forms of social science, and understanding the ethical, legal and institutional challenges involved, investigating the ways in which social factors shape the development of tools and technologies and are, in turn, impacted by them was also a key objective. The Digital Social Research Strategy resulted in nearly 50 projects at over 20 UK institutions and covered 6 dimensions:

- new data sources such as administrative, commercial and tracking data;
- methodological developments to take advantage of the new data and infrastructure capabilities;
- increased capability of tools, infrastructure and services;
- new studies of the impact of e-Social Science on research and understanding innovation pathways;
- new practices in working with an increasing range of digital information and collaborative tools and
- working at a new scale to include international and interdisciplinary collaborations in ways that were not previously possible.

A number of issues raised at that original workshop are developed through contributions to this special issue. First is using digital tools for research in educational contexts. This includes both software, whether dedicated data collection apps that run on Smartphones and tablet computers or more generic tools, such as Facebook and other social media websites, originally set up for a different purpose, and hardware, whether handheld or desktop. Educational contexts range from the formal such as online discussion tools associated with a college virtual learning environment to the informal, such as discussion in a 'chat room' or comments on a 'blog'. As web content continues to evolve and grow, opportunities for the use of digital tools have snowballed in recent years. In their early primer on *E-Research: Methods, Strategies, and Issues*, Anderson and Kanuka (2002) suggested that this was the likely result of four drivers: volume, of both activity and applications; velocity, the speed of change with emphasis on speed and throughput; variety, which refers to forms of communication, and interaction and value, which is directly related to quality. This issue of value raises questions of for whom, and for what, and leads to a deeper consideration of the second issue raised at the workshop: What are the benefits of online and digital tools for data collection and analysis and are there associated challenges?

Benefits outlined by Markausite and Reimer (2014) centre on the multitude of ways in which questions as to how people learn and particularly how they learn with technologies can now be explored both inside and outside formal learning environments using a range of digital tools. These tools encompass activities such as measuring brain activity, emotional responses and eye movement, advanced video-recording techniques, educational data mining, social network analysis and a range of other data-rich exploration, modelling and visualization techniques. Markausite and Reimer (2014) conclude that this leads to an increased range of possibilities to get deeper insight into learning phenomena and the complex relationships between them. At the same time, we need also to be mindful of challenges in their use such as the need to learn new, often complicated tools that rely on, occasionally erratic, Internet connectivity and how this increased depth of insight can impact on the relationships between researchers and participants when using online tools and digital technologies. This potential impact on the researcher and the researched was our third issue and is brought to the fore in projects that involve crossing boundaries such as those between home and school, work and social life, or informal and formal learning contexts. This is a feature of educational research via digital ethnography or in the evaluation of mobile learning opportunities where collecting data via the technology may influence the nature of the research and the researcher–participant relationship.

The fourth issue from the original workshop to be developed further in this special issue of the *International Journal of Research & Method in Education*, the roles of social media, connectedness and digital research, has led to significant challenges related to changes in the creation, co-production and dissemination of knowledge. Easier access to knowledge, the everyday use of highly portable mobile devices to access networked environments and the blurring of boundaries between private and public spheres, as well as between knowledge producer and knowledge consumer, have all resulted in opportunities and challenges that require careful consideration, reflection and elaboration vis-à-vis existing practices. This brings us to the fifth issue, the challenge to existing approaches to research ethics, for informed consent, anonymization and confidentiality require redefinition in the new social, political and cultural spaces involved in e-research.

One final issue that was intended to be raised at the original workshop, how is openness in the context of digital research understood and enacted in education, did not stimulate any contributions either to the workshop or to this special issue. Nor did we receive any submissions linked to big data and its associated new field of learning analytics. This leaves us concerned that there are unanswered questions and a real need to explore the pros, cons and ethical considerations of using technology 'behind the scenes' in schools or colleges to collect, analyse and store large data-sets.

Turning now to the special issue itself, we open with an article by Marina Wernholm and Sylvi Vigmo that pushes the boundaries of ethnography not so much into a minefield as into Minecraft, the massive, multiplayer online role-playing game in which participants use three-dimensional blocks to build constructions of all kinds, from small buildings to islands complete with cities and natural features such as forests and volcanoes, for example. They set out to explore how using online tools and digital technologies can influence data collection opportunities when researching online communities involving children with the aim of identifying a more holistic picture of the role of digital media in young people's everyday lives, especially regarding digital gaming among younger children. In response to the known challenges of digital ethnography, such as those highlighted by Hammersley (2006) – we do not know who the creators of online contributions are, what their purposes were nor what their circumstances are, beyond what is posted online – they involved children known to each other and the researchers as research collaborators. The children decided which of their gameplay sessions in Minecraft to record and share with the researchers, their parents. While this paper focuses on the challenges of digital ethnography, it also introduces us to a potentially useful online data collection tool, FRAPS, a real-time video capture software that enables players to record their play sessions while gaming. On screen conversations in the chat overlaying the constructions is captured alongside the gameplay and Wernholm and Vigmo use a theoretical framework informed by Vygotskian theories of mediation and language as a tool in the development of thinking to analyse the children's discussions.

This is followed by Sarah Parsons, Karen Guldberg, Kaska Porayska-Pomsta and Rachael Lee's informative and moving account of working with school practitioners in the co-creation of digital stories in a project focusing on embedding innovative uses for digital technologies for children on the autism spectrum into classroom practice. They hoped to find a way to bridge the known gap between research evidence and real-world teaching experience (Menter et al. 2010) which is particularly acute in the field of research addressing educational interventions for children with autism where studies are often undertaken in laboratory settings rather than in classrooms (Parsons et al. 2013). Thus their aim was to use digital storytelling as a means to empower teachers to construct and share their own authentic narratives and to build case examples of creative technology-enhanced teaching and learning. The teachers' digital stories, consisting of short video narrative of approximately three to five minutes duration, were well received and celebrated within their school, one that makes specialist provision for children from the ages of 4 to 19 with autism. On the other hand, the researchers' experiences also show that not all teachers and schools may be ready for this type of knowledge co-creation. Even the school discussed here was initially unsure about the co-creation of digital stories due to space and logistical constraints, as well as concerns about fulfilling the research team's expectations. Parsons et al. explain this with reference to McFadyen and Cannella's (2004) point that in knowledge creation, information exchange is often emergent with collaborators being unable to articulate, a priori, the specific knowledge that they need. They conclude that in the case of digital storytelling, this emergent property of knowledge co-creation can 'offer creativity, support risk-taking and can develop agency and empowerment, but it can also be felt as uncomfortable, unsure and perhaps too risky in an environment where pressure on schools and teachers to meet standards is substantial' (2015, 267). They found that, overall, the process of engagement with the school, via the development of digital stories, was powerful, informative and challenging. The stories themselves could be viewed as artefacts evidencing the research and its impact that reflect local contexts, demonstrate e-inclusion practices (Abbott 2007) and foster opportunities for reflection and critique.

With the next paper, authored by Patricio Herbst, we move away from working with young people to focus on research into innovative methods for the education and training of their teachers. Herbst writes in detail about how he and his colleagues have developed the use of multimedia scenarios (e.g. storyboards and animations of non-descript cartoon characters delivered online) in research into professional knowledge. This knowledge is hard to access as it is so often tacit or held as part of a group (Cook and Brown 1999). Herbst's aim is to study what professionals, in this case maths teachers, notice and decide to do in practice systematically, in ways that improve upon earlier uses of written representations of professional scenarios or video-recorded episodes. He introduces us to the concept of a virtual, breaching experiment that originates in how ethnomethodologists have worked to understand the tacit order beneath the routine and everyday practice by hypothesizing about naturalized assumptions. Their hypotheses are then tested by immersing participants in instances of those practices where some of the norms under study are 'breached' and observing how the participants repair (i.e. notice, elaborate) the situation. These virtual, breaching experiments comprise animations of classroom scenarios, where teacher and students were represented using non-descript cartoon characters voiced over by human actors (Herbst, Nachlieli, and Chazan 2011). A particular advantage is that, not being limited to finding or recording video, the researchers could script lesson scenarios in order to control how the norms being studied would be breached. These multimedia scenarios can easily be linked to an online questionnaire to gather data on participants' possible responses to the 'breach' in the scenario through attitude scales or through ranking them in order of preference. Another advantage is that having animated characters enables multimodal representation of human activity in context which ensures the face validity of the associated questions.

Continuing with the theme of e-research as a way of exploring professional development for educators, we next have Daniel Kilburn and Jonathan Earley's paper on using Disqus, a web-based commenting platform, for a study into the teaching and learning of social research methods. They had noted that comparatively little research has engaged directly with the question of how social science research is taught and learnt as part of the academic career (Kilburn, Nind, and Wiles 2014) and aimed to address this gap. In their paper, they examine the challenges and opportunities arising from the development of web-based commenting as an adaptation of online focus-group methods to engage doctoral and ECR learners in social sciences across the UK in dialogue over how research methods are taught and learnt. For this purpose, they developed an e-research method that utilized website-based commenting via an already popular platform called Disqus that could be integrated into an existing web-page design. Also known as integrated online discussion forums (Birch and Weitkamp 2010), website-based commenting facilities have become a popular means for web users to post anonymous or pseudonymous comments in response to news articles, blogs, social media and other web content. Kilburn and Earley go on to discuss how this tool provided the researchers with both quantitative paradata such as number of page-views and time spent on each and rich comments to qualitatively analyse. The latter were particularly useful with a number of contributions offering a greater level of depth, detail or consideration than might be expected from a face-to-face discussion. That said, we note that their data collection illustrates one of the hazards of e-research, they recruited low numbers of participants despite emailing their request to comment to thousands of academics who shared an interest in social science research methodology.

The following paper, authored by Margaret Walshaw and Wayne Duncan, describes a much richer way forward for online data collection rather than simply using comments or messages as records of online collaboration. Their research centres on investigating the role of empathy in teaching and learning. Empathy is central to knowledge development for, 'without empathic abilities or limited abilities of social actors to empathize, new meanings become difficult to construct' (2014, 306). Yet observing, even signalling, empathy in distance education, that is, an educational environment usually without face-to-face interaction is extremely challenging. However, the authors had noted the introduction of synchronous, multimedia conferencing tools such as Adobe Connect which enable real-time voice, video, text and application sharing within multipoint, distributed learner environments. Access to this flexible, interactive and content-rich software enabled them to continue their research, aiming to understand both the role of empathy in teaching and learning and students' and teachers' experiences of this phenomenon, in the context of distance education. Their paper itself focuses on how following the principles of hermeneutics enabled the authors to take a methodological stance that initiated a cycle of understanding and allowed them to remain faithful to participants' evaluations of empathy in online environments. They conclude that taking a hermeneutic approach enhances an understanding of empathy when synchronous, multimedia conferencing is used in educational contexts.

Ethical issues alluded to in the above articles – unseen collaborators in gameplay, unattributable comments on discussion boards, unknown reasons behind making a comment, uncertainty about the affordances of new technologies, publishing video that includes children and the difficulty of maintaining confidentiality of participants, especially those under age, who self-publish their details online – alert us to the emerging ethical issues of online and digital tool use mentioned in the opening of this editorial. We therefore conclude this special issue with Trish Andrews, Laurel Dyson and Jocelyn Wishart's discussion of scenario generation as a way of supporting researchers with the need to consider ethics of e-research in educational contexts. They take a particular interest in research in schools and classrooms that involves students' use of mobile devices that connect with social media and note that the researchers involved may include teachers researching their own practice. They present the latest version of an ethics framework originally formulated by Wishart (2009) by cross-tabulating issues of students' use of mobile devices and social media giving rise to concern in schools and colleges with accepted ethical principles in order to scaffold discussion and scenario generation in professional development workshops and seminars.

Following up this focus on ethical concerns, we include a review of the new edition of Mark Israel's book *Research Ethics and Integrity for Social Scientists: Beyond Regulatory Compliance* by Debby Watson. It aims to revisit the work of the first edition through updated and extended coverage of issues relating to international, indigenous, interdisciplinary and, of course, Internet research. We also include a review by Professor Steve Higgins on the extensive *Sage Handbook of Digital Technology Research* published in 2013 and edited by Sara Price, Carey Jewitt and Barry Brown. Its third section, 'Research Perspectives for Digital Technologies: Theory and Analysis', includes chapters on ethnographic and multimodal methods in digital technology research and is particularly relevant to this issue.

We complete the review section and the Special Issue itself with Christian Bokhove's appraisal of the freely available *Lesson Note* app, created by the Lesson Study Alliance, which enables lesson observers to create visual depictions of classrooms and classroom layouts with students, desks or tables, groups, teachers and displays to support note taking. A particularly useful feature is the ability to 'swipe' between entities to record interactions making it suitable for analysing classroom interaction patterns and social network analysis.

Finally, to return to the original questions to be tackled through the publication of this special issue, how are digital innovations changing the way we think about research? How is research in the digital age being conducted? And what are the consequent implications for how we conceptualize education? In attempting to answer these questions, it has become clear that both education and educational research now often involve:

- crossing, even shattering, boundaries such as those between informal and formal learning contexts or between the virtual and the real, both in space and in time;
- the increasing use of multimedia and other visual learning tools foregrounding multimodal opportunities in both teaching and research;
- expectations as to digital literacy on all parties involved, the students, their teachers or lecturers and educational researchers, and
- issues of responsibility, ethics and approaches to inculcating ethical awareness with particular attention to the ease with which information and images can be sent across the world and into thousands of homes, whether on purpose or through accident or a lack of foresight.

We hope that this special issue will contribute to existing debates about these methodological and ethical questions and promote further opportunities for discussion among the journal's readership in the future.

References

Abbott, C. 2007. *E-Inclusion: Learning Difficulties and Digital Technologies*. Bristol: Futurelab. Accessed August 5, 2014 www.futurelab.org.uk.

Anderson, T., and E. Kanuka. 2002. *eResearch: Methods, Strategies and Issues*. Boston, MA: Allyn & Bacon.

Birch, H., and E. Weitkamp. 2010. "Podologues: Conversations Created by Science Podcasts." *New Media & Society* 12 (6): 889–909.

Cook, S. D., and J. S. Brown. 1999. "Bridging Epistemologies: The Generative Dance between Organizational Knowledge and Organizational Knowing." *Organization Science* 10 (4): 381–400.

ESRC. 2012. Digital Social Research Strategy. Accessed March 05, 2015. http://www.esrc.ac.uk/_images/DSR%20strategy_tcm8-19855.pdf

Greenhow, C., B. Robelia, and J. E. Hughes. 2009. "Learning, Teaching, and Scholarship in a Digital Age: Web 2.0 and Classroom Research: What Path Should We Take Now?" *Educational Researcher* 38 (4): 246–259. doi: $10.3102/0013189 \times 09336671$

Hammersley, M. 2006. "Ethnography: Problems and Prospects." *Ethnography and Education* 1 (1): 3–14 doi: 10.1080/17457820500512697

Herbst, P., T. Nachlieli, and D. Chazan. 2011. "Studying the Practical Rationality of Mathematics Teaching: What Goes into "Installing" a Theorem in Geometry?" *Cognition and Instruction* 29 (2): 1–38.

Kilburn, D., M. Nind, and R. Wiles. 2014. "Learning as Researchers and Teachers: The Development of a Pedagogical Culture for Social Science Research Methods?" *British Journal of Educational Studies* 62 (2): 191–207.

Markauskaite, L., and P. Reimann. 2014. "Editorial: e-Research for Education: Applied, Methodological and Critical Perspectives." *British Journal of Educational Technology* 45: 385–391. doi: 10.1111/bjet.12154

McFadyen, M. A., and A. A. Cannella, Jr. 2004. "Social Capital and Knowledge Creation: Diminishing Returns of the Number and Strength of Exchange Relationships." *The Academy of Management Journal,* 47 (5): 735–746.

Menter, I., M. Hulme, J. Murray, A. Campbell, I. Hextall, M. Jones, P. Mahony, R. Procter, and K. Wall. 2010. "Teacher Education Research in the UK: The State of the Art." *Schweizerische Zeitschrift für Bildungswissenschaften* 32 (1): 121–142.

Parsons, S., T. Charman, R. Faulkner, J. Ragan, S. Wallace, and K. Wittemeyer. 2013. "Bridging the Research and Practice Gap in Autism: The Importance of Creating Research Partnerships with Schools." *Autism* 17 (3): 268–280.

Parsons, S., K. Guldberg, K. Porayska-Pomsta, and R. Lee. 2015. "Digital Stories as a Method for Evidence-based Practice and Knowledge Co-creation in Technology-enhanced Learning for Children with Autism." *International Journal of Research & Method in Education*. doi: 10.1080/1743727X.2015.1019852

Walshaw, M., and W. Duncan. 2014. "Hermeneutics as a Methodological Resource for Understanding Empathy in On-line Learning Environments." *International Journal of Research & Method in Education*. doi: 10.1080/1743727X.2014.914166

Wishart, J. 2009. "Ethical Considerations in Implementing Mobile Learning in the Workplace." *International Journal of Mobile and Blended Learning* 1 (2): 76–92.

Jocelyn Wishart
University of Bristol, Bristol, UK

Michael Thomas
University of Central Lancashire, Preston, UK

Capturing children's knowledge-making dialogues in Minecraft

Marina Wernholm[a] and Sylvi Vigmo[b]

[a]Department of Education, The Linnaeus University, Kalmar, Sweden; [b]Department of Education, Communication and Learning, University of Gothenburg, Gothenburg, Sweden

The aim of this article is to address how online tools and digital technologies can influence data collection opportunities. We are still at the early stages of piecing together a more holistic picture of the role of digital media in young people's everyday lives, especially regarding digital gaming among younger children. Digital technologies have enabled both new ways of gaming together and the possibility of capturing children's everyday knowledge-making dialogues in a non-institutionalized digital environment. In this case study, the online tool FRAPS®, which enables players to record their play sessions while gaming was used to address data collection opportunities. By using this tool, the lifeworlds of children could be displayed through their knowledge-making dialogues, which also captured the resources the children use when they collaboratively played Minecraft. The analysis draws on peer learning and on Vygotsky's notions of object-regulation, other-regulation and self-regulation. The results show that language was a resource when the children collaboratively played, Minecraft® online, as enabling *other-regulation*. Other resources of importance connected to language use were digital tools and artefacts, such as computers, headsets, Skype and smartphones, *object-regulation*. The children's previous knowledge and experiences from their ordinary lifeworld used in the game also became resources. The resources can also be built into the game and regarded as affordances. The children already know how many of these affordances are used, *self-regulation*, and external assistance did not seem necessary.

Introduction

The beginning of the twenty-first century has been called *the age of digitalization* (Takahasi 2010, 2). Researchers are still seeking to make sense of the role of Internet in a changing world (Markham and Baym 2009). Our values and norms concerning public participation, literacy and education are being challenged by a rapidly shifting landscape of media and communication in which children are central actors (Ito et al. 2009). Young people's relationships with digital technology are still under discussion, regarding benefits (Buckingham 2006; Selwyn 2009; Thorne, Fischer, and Lu 2012) as well as fears (Brandtzaeg and Stav 2004; Wartella and Jennings 2010). There are fears of children losing their childhood and becoming passive and isolated due to the use of computer games and other media technologies (Brandtzaeg et al.

2004; Lindahl and Folkesson 2012). There are, however, other arguments raised, for example, that many play activities nowadays take place in digital online environments, the children's new playground (Linderoth, Björk, and Olsson 2014). Miller and Horst (2012), refer to Boellstorff who argues that online worlds are simply another arena, alongside offline worlds, for expressive practice and that no one arena is privileged over the other.

During the last decade, digital gaming has become increasingly popular, for example, games played via screens like those on computers or portable devices (Bennerstedt 2013). Digital gaming activities and practices have their own unique characteristics, and new ways of gaming together have been established (Bennerstedt 2013). These particular ways of gaming are of interest in this study since the activity takes place in non-institutionalized digital environments. Thorne, Black, and Sykes (2009) argue that what occurs online, outside of instructed educational settings, involves extended periods of language socialization, adaptation and creative semiotic work that illustrate vibrant communicative practices. At the same time, due to technological mediation, our everyday linguistic and social practices undergo significant shifts (Thorne, Black, and Sykes 2009). However, in order to fully understand the lifeworlds of children, researchers must turn to a variety of settings; home, online and together with other children. That means moving into more private spheres compared with doing educational ethnography (Mackay 2005).

Aim

The aim of this article is to address how online tools and digital technologies can influence data collection opportunities. In this case study, the online tool FRAPS®, which enables players to record their play sessions while playing Minecraft®, will be used to address data collection opportunities. Minecraft® is a multiplayer sandbox construction game focused on creativity, building and survival and can be played on multiplayer servers and single-player worlds across multiple game modes. The following questions are of interest: How can FRAPS® be used to collect data when researching children's knowledge-making dialogues? How can the resources the children use when they collaboratively play Minecraft® be captured?

Research overview

Ethnography – yesterday and today?

An ethnographer is always in need for a gatekeeper in order to gain access to the field (Cohen, Manion, and Morrison 2009; Walford 2008a). Gaining access is one of the most problematic aspects when it comes to conducting ethnography research and can only proceed where access has been achieved (Walford 2008a, 2008b). Adler and Adler (1996) point to one of the advantages they experienced by using their own children as gatekeepers. Their membership role in the community to which their children belonged, offered them a naturalness and ease of access, which they would not otherwise have had. The same experience was found in this case study. However, community itself is a concept that is widely used in different contexts and the definition therefore has become quite blurred and widely debated (Guimaraes 2005; Kozinets 2010). In this case study, Minecraft players using the same server are regarded as a community.

There are difficult issues in the area of ethnographic research, to mention some of them; how ethnographers define the spatial and temporal boundaries of what they study; how they determine the context that is appropriate for understanding it, in what senses ethnography can be – or is – virtual rather than actual (Hammersley 2006). However, Hammersley emphasizes the importance of studying *at first hand* what people do and say in a particular context. Walford (2008b) claims that an ethnographer docs not scck the unusual, rather writes about the routine daily lives of people. This case study aims to keep to the essence of ethnography, as expressed by Hammersley (2006, 11) as 'the tension between trying to understand people's perspectives from the inside while also viewing them and their behavior more distantly'. According to Walford (2008b), ethnographers stress that they move within social worlds, and in order to understand the behaviour, values and meaning of any group, ethnographers must take their cultural context into account. The word culture in relation to ethnography can be understood as: 'A culture is made up of certain values, practices, relationships and identifications' (Walford 2008b, 7). We apply the following definition of context in this article: 'Context refers not just to space and time but also to the various parameters of human interaction with digital technologies, which form part of material practice' (Miller and Horst 2012, 27). The cultural context in this case study is Minecraft®.

In earlier years, fieldwork took place over a long period of time (Hammersley 2006). Fieldwork today, however, is more likely to last weeks rather than years due to various factors, for example, the shortening of contracts for researchers employed on particular projects and an increasing pressure on academics for productivity. Another factor of importance is the use of audio- and video-recording devices that can produce very large amounts of data material quite rapidly (Hammersley 2006). The online tool FRAPS®[1] was used in this case study to capture the knowledge-making dialogues. A more specific issue to be discussed is whether there can be such a concept as Internet or virtual ethnography. In the case of virtual ethnography all the data are commonly available and collected online without meeting people face to face. Studies of communities online take a particular social or communal phenomenon as their focal area of interest, for example, Minecraft®. Through the study of an online community, something significant can be learnt about the wider focal community, their behaviour, its participants and their values or beliefs (Kozinets 2010). Hence, Hammersley (2006, 8) raises the question: 'Are there online cultures that can be studied by Internet ethnographers?' On the one hand, there are severe limitations to Internet data from a traditional ethnographic point of view. On the other hand, it can be argued that people today obviously display enough about themselves through their participation to enable ethnographic studies of online practices (Hammersley 2006, 8). Therefore, the use of digital technologies in social and educational research can be discussed as both opportunities to be grasped and threats to be countered (Hine 2005).

Other issues are addressed by MacCallum-Stewart (2013) who argues that player activity is developing so fast that cohesive studies are very difficult to present. Moreover, gamers produce new texts with rapidity, which is hard to follow for researchers, one of the consequences being that there is a lack of research in this area. Gamers are natural early adopters of technologies and therefore use a diverse series of tools across media and methods to express ideas about gaming (MacCallum-Stewart 2013). To sum up, online social formations seem to challenge existing ways of conceptualizing research sites and ask for new strategies of exploration (Hine 2005; Kozinets 2010).

FRAPS® – a tool for exploration that provides opportunities

Digital technologies have enabled the possibility of capturing children's everyday dialogues in a non-institutionalized digital environment. In this case study, the online tool FRAPS®, which enables players to record their play sessions while gaming, was used to address and explore data collection opportunities. The children in this study are telling their own story in their own way, from their perspective. Moreover, all the participants were well aware that the researchers were going to analyse their dialogues. Coppock's (2011) key argument for participatory approaches is that, by privileging children's voice, researchers facilitate access to authentic knowledge about children's subjective realities and empower the children to promote their agency. This is in line with Grover who draws the following conclusion in her article:

> What is clear from the academic study of children is that children have been virtually excluded as active participants in the research process; treated rather as 'objects of study'. When children are permitted in those rare cases to become active participants telling their own story in their own way, the research experience is often personally moving and meaningful and the data provided rich and complex. (2004, 84)

One can draw upon Articles 12 and 13 (UN 1989) in relation to research involving children. The content in the articles includes the right for children to be involved in decision-making processes and to receive and impart information in a manner that matches their self-identified competence (UN 1989). The children in this study were initially informed that they had the right to decide which of the recorded play sessions they wanted to share with the researchers. Mortari and Harcourt (2012) argue that the aim for a researcher is not to find a solution for ethical dilemmas since this could be regarded as an impossible task. Rather, it is more about living ethical dilemmas when researching with children (Mortari and Harcourt 2012; Phelan and Kinsella 2013). In line with Nutbrown who calls for reflexivity, as researchers, we need to examine 'our own positionality, what brings us to the project, and what we really think about children' (2010, 11). We have to be clear about our values which eventually will affect the importance we give to children's actions and views and above all we need to address how useful their view of the world is (Nutbrown 2010). The study presented here, aimed at capturing the children's view of the world in Minecraft® by exploring their knowledge-making dialogues, when they collaboratively play Minecraft.

The cultural context: Minecraft®

Currently, a huge populace exists around Minecraft® and its developer Mojang AB stresses that endorsement and publicity of their game have arisen entirely from community development, not from marketing. The result is that over seven million people have bought Minecraft® since its release in 2009 (MacCallum-Stewart 2013). Minecraft® was created by Markus 'Notch' Persson and is a multiplayer sandbox construction game focused on creativity, building and survival. The game involves players controlling an avatar that can break and place various types of blocks in a three-dimensional environment that consists completely of blocks. Blocks represent different materials, such as dirt and stone. The players must acquire resources and survive a hostile environment and must maintain their health and hunger at acceptable levels or the avatar might die or drop all the items in the inventory. The inventory is a pop-up menu that the player uses to manage items. Minecraft® can be played on multiplayer servers and single-player worlds across multiple game modes with four alternatives: *creative*, where players have unlimited resources, there are no threats and the avatar can fly freely; *survival*, where players are challenged by life-threatening creatures every night, must search for resources, craft items, and can gain levels; *adventure*, which is almost like survival mode, but the player needs tools to break things and *hardcore*, similar to survival, but players only have one life (Canossa, Martinez, and Togelius 2013; MacCallum-Stewart 2013). Minecraft® is possibly one of the oddest hits ever according to Leavitt (2011). Firstly, because it gained a huge approbation from a community longing to be listened to and secondly because Minecraft® does not rely on micro-transactional payments in order to succeed, unlike many other virtual worlds (MacCallum-Stewart 2013). Minecraft® affords possibilities for expressing curiosity and players have a wide range of ways to investigate, research and create.

The changing face of gaming culture

The development of digital technology has accelerated enormously and there have been significant changes in media during this age (Ito et al. 2009). One is the growth of CGM (consumer-generated media) such as YouTube®, SNS (social networking sites) and COI (community of interest) (Takahasi 2010). Some researchers (Turkle 2011) criticize social media, arguing that the negative things that take place on social media networks may result in a sense of increased isolation. This case study aims to address the opposite case; that is, regarding YouTube® as a resource and a relatively new contact zone for the digital gaming community to gain more knowledge and actually watch recorded play sessions (Golub 2010; Lange 2008; MacCallum-Stewart 2013). YouTube® has become a powerful space, a resource that not only affords new ways to consume, create and share video clips, but also allows the players to refine, augment and transform their craft (Cayari 2011). Additionally, player-developed tools such as FRAPS® and Audacity®, which capture video and commentary by the player as the game is played, have made recording increasingly easy. Therefore, a walkthrough is much more easily explained when the viewer actually sees what the player is doing. This cross-pollination, in which the players take an active part in the game and then demonstrate it to others, is a relatively new phenomenon (MacCallum-Stewart 2013). According to Leavitt (2011), players' commitment to the game leads them to engage in knowledge-making activities outside the game world. A parallel can be drawn from a case study about teenage musicians, which describes how YouTube® has affected music consumption, creation and sharing to a wider community (Cayari 2011). The YouTube® users had developed a community in which technology had enabled new kinds of musical creativity. In the same way, YouTube® has affected the Minecraft® gaming culture regarding consumption, creation and sharing, but also in how technology has enabled new kinds of creativity in Minecraft® to spread. 'With no doubt, these sites are changing the content distribution landscape and even the popular culture' (Cheng, Liu, and Dale 2013, 1184). Furthermore, the more committed a group is to a project, the more likely that the project is to spread to other parts of these children's lifeworlds (Lange 2008). It has been argued that there are two purposes with children sharing video clips; the first is that they want other children to learn and improve their craft, the second is that they want to gain recognition and reputation and an audience for their creative work (Ito et al. 2009). Between August 2010 and March 2011, the number of Minecraft® videos on YouTube® went from 4000 to over 800,000 according to the Pax Panel website, 25 May 2014. Technology affects the way people create, consume and share art, media and performance: 'the users of technology shape the technology's purpose as the technology shapes the users' culture' (Cayari 2011, 6). To conclude, players take an active role in the development and dissemination of Minecraft®, which in turn is changing the ways in which the game is interpreted (MacCallum-Stewart 2013).

Theoretical framework

Video sharing sites, such as YouTube®, might be described as vast constellations of artefacts and human resources supporting processes associated with the zone of proximal development (ZPD), drawing upon Vygotskian developmental theory (Thorne 2012). Taking a sociocultural perspective, we as researchers will adopt the three following concepts originally put forward by Vygotsky, to describe a developmentally sequenced shift in the locus of control of human activity to regulate thinking: object-regulation, other-regulation and self-regulation (Thorne 2012; Thorne, Black, and Sykes 2009). When artefacts in the environment afford or make possible cognition/activity, object-regulation is used to describe the instances (Thorne and Tasker 2011). This can be exemplified by the use of a headset and a portable device in order to be able to communicate with players online while gaming. Other-regulation (Thorne and Tasker 2011) refers to mediation by other people, such as supportive comments, linguistic feedback or guidance from an expert. Self-regulation refers to individuals, for whom external assistance is largely unnecessary. That is because originally external forms of mediation have been internalized and are therefore no longer needed for execution or completion of a task. Thus, self-regulated individuals can serve as models and mentors (Thorne, Black, and Sykes 2009). Development can be described as the process of gaining greater voluntary control over one's capacity to think and act, either by becoming more proficient in the use of meditational resources, or by relying less on external meditational means (Thorne and Tasker 2011; Vygotsky 1986).

Vygotskian framework for analysing online communities

Thorne (2012) used a model to analyse second language (L2) fan fiction writing based on Vygotskian developmental theory (1986) and drawing upon the concepts object-, other-, and self-regulation. Fan fiction authors borrowed from original media and received reviews from fellow authors, which led to improvement of their own writing. Of importance was that the fan fiction authors had a reason to do so, namely an attentive audience of peers, and the affirmation through responses. The authors were contributing to a collective enterprise through their authorial contributions. In this study, we draw on Thorne's model (Thorne 2012, 310) (Figure 1) to analyse online gaming communities: the single player plays the digital game and receives feedback from the community and improves his/her knowledge in gaming. Players publish their video recordings on YouTube® and contribute to the collective enterprise, which enables single players to seek more knowledge by watching clips and to improve their gaming (Golub 2010; Ito et al. 2009).

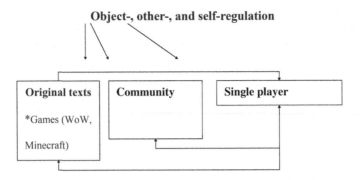

Figure 1.   Object-, other-, and self-regulation draw on Thorne (2012).

Method

One of the researchers became interested in Minecraft® due to having a child who spent much time on playing. This led to questions like: What is Minecraft®? What is so special about Minecraft®? Before starting the data collection for this study, one could say that the researcher actually lived in the field, together with a Minecraft® player for six months. During that time, further questions were raised: How can they play together without meeting? Why do Minecraft players watch clips on YouTube? What different kinds of clips can be found on YouTube? These six months also included online research fieldwork watching a variety of Minecraft® clips uploaded on YouTube. The results in this case study are built on these six months of fieldwork and video footage from focused game playing sessions together with examples from more in-depth dialogues to address the research questions.

A case study provides a unique example of real people in real situations (Cohen, Manion, and Morrison 2009). In this case study, the children were interacting with each other online by using Skype while gaming, without being in the same physical space. The programme FRAPS® made it possible to capture the children's everyday knowledge-making dialogues in the non-institutionalized digital environment of Minecraft®. One of the children in the study was already familiar with how to use FRAPS®, and could therefore be involved in the process of collecting the data. However, only one computer screen was recorded, and the dialogues among the three players are thus captured through the recording of that one player's screen. A researcher needs to reflect upon how data collection might alter the behaviour of the participants (Heath, Hindmarsh, and Luff 2011). By using this method, data could be collected without interference or disturbance from the researchers and the lifeworlds of children playing Minecraft could be captured on site. The children were active participants telling their own story in their own way, which eventually provided rich and complex data for analysis. The data consist of four recorded play sessions as follows:

(1) Minecraft® 1.1 Length of clip 17:33 min (player 1, player 2 and player 3)
(2) Minecraft® 3:1 Length of clip: 14:49 min (player 1, player 2 and player 3)
(3) Minecraft® 1 Length of clip: 14:43 min (player 1 and player 2)
(4) Minecraft® 2 Length of clip: 11:59 min (player 1 and player 2)

In the initial stage of analysing the data, all the play sessions were watched on a computer. Clips were paused and notes were taken by hand, both on what the children were talking about and the time when the dialogue took place. In the next step, the dialogues were transcribed in more detail in Swedish on a computer, marking the time for ease of going back and forth in the material during the analysis. One of the children acted as an interpreter during the transcription process, since the children used special game-related concepts which were not familiar to the researchers. A two-column system was used, with the transcripts to the left and space for notes to the right. The transcripts were then analysed from the question: Which of all these dialogues can be characterized as knowledge-making dialogues? Knowledge making is used here to define that the children create, spread and share knowledge, which eventually becomes part of their collective enterprise. The dialogues that were not identified as knowledge making were left out from further analysis. Furthermore, the remaining dialogues were analysed based on the question: Which resources do the children use in these knowledge-making dialogues? The interpretations were written in the right column. Thirdly, the search for categories started and three main categories were found: *Crossing Between Languages, Previous Knowledge and Experiences Become Resources in Minecraft*® and *Resources Connected to Minecraft*®. Finally, the units of analysis of object-, other-, and self-regulation from the theoretical framework were applied, also written in the right column.

All the participants in the study were under age according to the Swedish Research Council[2] (2011), that is, under the age of 15, so a letter of informed consent was distributed to their parents. From an ethical point of view, there are still many issues to be discussed in this area, especially since the guidelines of informed consent can be widely interpreted when conducting research online (Kozinets 2010). However, research may be unethical even though performed with informed consent, and sometimes research may not be unethical even though performed without informed consent (Sveningsson Elm 2009). Cohen, Manion, and Morrison (2009) argue that research contexts are unique and dynamic. Furthermore, a case study investigates and reports the complex dynamic and unfolds interactions of events, human relationships and other factors in a unique example (Cohen, Manion, and Morrison (2009)).

Results

The aim of this article is to address how online tools and digital technologies can influence data collection opportunities. The following questions are of interest: How can FRAPS® be used to collect data when researching children's knowledge-making dialogues? How can the resources the children use when they collaboratively play Minecraft® be captured?

The children's interactions in Swedish are described and discussed connected to excerpts, which have been translated and are displayed here in a different font in English. The words spoken in English by the children are written in bold to clearly show the children's crossing between languages.

Crossing between languages

The results from the captured knowledge-making dialogues show that language is a resource when the children collaboratively play Minecraft® online, that is, *other-regulation*. Through language use, the players gain and share knowledge since the community gains when the players become better to collaborate with. The constant flow in the dialogues is striking and also notable is the variation of what they actually express while gaming. The use of language, *self-regulation*, can be regarded as a condition for taking part in the online activity. In order to participate in a community, a player needs to know the game-related concepts and language used while gaming. Other resources of importance connected to language use that the children address are digital tools and artefacts, *object-regulation*, such as computers, headsets, Skype and smartphones. Their knowledge-making dialogues are captured and mediated by cultural artefacts for Internet communication, using tools such as Skype. When there is a disruption in the mediation due to technology problems, they express irritation. When a player in the community does not know what to do, he asks the others for help, *other-regulation,* to gain more knowledge. Excerpt 1 below is an example of the ZPD (Vygotsky 1986), that is what an individual can accomplish in a joint activity when provided with assistance by someone more knowledgeable:

Excerpt 1.

Player 2:	Vänta man ska inte ha **fancy** va
	Wait you shouldn' t have **fancy** eh
Player 1:	Nej det ska man inte
	No you shouldn' t
Player 2:	Är det grafik snabbt?
	Are there graphics quickly
Player 1:	Ja snabbt ... det har jag för då **laggar** det mycket mindre
	Yes quickly ... I use that because then it doesn' t **lag** so much

A phenomenon which clearly stands out in the children's knowledge-making dialogues throughout all the play sessions is the constant crossing between languages, a mix between the Swedish language and English concepts. All the children are native Swedish speakers and English is the first foreign language taught in school. They mainly use Swedish in their dialogues, but there is a recurrent use of English concepts. Their language is full of specific concepts and jargon, especially when they address resources or artefacts, which are used in Minecraft®. The children make Swedish verbs out of English verbs, by transferring the Swedish grammar structure, *self-regulation.*

An example of how digital tools and artefacts, *object-regulation*, do not only mediate communication and uses of literacy, concerns how they re-mediate existing human activity to create new morphologies of action. The children's dialogues are sometimes impossible to understand for someone not a member of the community, and one of the children had the interpreter's role in the analytical process of the captured dialogue. The dialogue, in Excerpt 2, is also an example of how they constantly share their experiences while gaming.

Excerpt 2.

Player 2:	Alltså har du någonsin **failat** ... typ gjort asmånga **buttons**
	Well have you ever **failed** ... like done plenty of **buttons**
Player 1:	ja det gjorde jag ... jag gjorde ...
	Yes I did ... I did ...
Player 2:	Jag skulle typ göra något annat skit och gjorde jag typ 4 **stacks** med **buttons** och så gjorde jag typ en **stack** med **pressure place** också

```
                  Like I should do some other shit and I did like 4
                  stacks with buttons and I did like one stack with
                  pressure place as well
```
Player 1:   På **Feed the beast** gjorde jag så ... fast jag hade en **product table** ... typ som om man lägger i någonting så gör man det så kan man trycka och få ut asmånga typ. Det man har i **inventoryt** eller vad man säger ... så då typ hade jag asmånga **stacks** ... typ 15 **stacks** med knappar
```
                  At Feed the beast I did so ...but I had a product table
                  ...like if you put one thing inside it then you can
                  push and get plenty of the same thing. The things
                  you have got in the inventory or what you say..like
                  then I had plenty of stacks..like 15 stacks with
                  buttons
```

Meta-conversations about language are also captured in the children's knowledge-making dialogues. Player 1 initiates one of the meta-conversations, about their crossing between languages. He wants comments from the others, *other-regulation*. As exemplified in Excerpt 3, playing online means meeting other players and exchanging different kinds of experiences.

Excerpt 3.

Player 1:   men vissa grejer på Minecraft® säger man på svenska och vissa på engelska
```
                  But some things on Minecraft® you say in Swedish and
                  some things in English
```
Player 3:   ja det är konstigt
```
                  Yes it's strange
```
Player 2:   t typ **chest** säger jag och **piston** så men spade säger jag spade ... och **picker** säger man ju också på engelska ju
```
                  Like chest I say chest sort of and piston but shovel I say
                  ... and picker you also say in English
```
Player 3:   ja typ
```
                  yes sort of
```

Previous knowledge and experiences become resources in Minecraft®

The children's previous knowledge and experiences from their ordinary lifeworld are captured in their knowledge-making dialogues and can be regarded as resources, which are used in the game. Minecraft® affords possibilities for expressing curiosity and players have a wide range of ways to investigate, research and create. Obviously, it is possible to construct so-called cowboy buildings also in the Minecraft®-world and Player 1 and Player 2 have both done that. In Sweden, there is a TV programme 'Fusk-byggarna'/'The Cowboy builders' which Player 2 knows of. The dialogue takes place while Player 1 is building the roof of a house, as seen in Excerpt 4.

Excerpt 4.

Player 1:   Jag bygger på mitt tak. Jag har ett riktigt fuskbygge här för jag typ byggt så att jag inte slösar på **wood**
```
                  I'm building my roof. I have got a real cowboy build-
                  ing here because I have built it so that I don't waste
                  wood
```

Player 2:   Då kommer det vara typ inåtlutande grejer
             Then it will be like a reverse slope
Player 1:   Jag vet, men det kommer inte synas
             I know, but no one will see it
Player 2:   (skrattar) ... jag har fuskbyggt också
             (laughs) ... I have also been cowboy building
Player 1:   Har du också fuskat?
             Have you also cheated?
Player 2:   Någon kommer anmäla mig till 'Fuskbyggarna'
             Someone will report me to 'The Cowboy Builders'

Knowledge and experiences from the ordinary context can also be directly applied to the Minecraft® world. In other words, the conditions can be the same in both worlds. Another knowledge-making dialogue captures the importance of air in order to survive under water. The dialogue also includes discussing which artefact, *object-regulation*, keeps control over the air. The conditions are also the same when it comes to material for construction. Oakwood is better to use for construction than junglewood. Player 2 makes clear in the captured dialogue that the chests will be of better quality if oakwood is used.

Resources connected to Minecraft®

The resources such as TNT, which stands for TriNitroToluene, can be used to blow things up, and night vision potion which is used to be able to see in the dark can also be built into the game and present opportunities for actions which can be regarded as affordances, which are implicit in the captured knowledge-making dialogues. In the analysis of data, one of the children makes clear that the community plays in the Survival easy mode that enables players to see the resources and utilize their affordances. The knowledge-making dialogues show that the children know how many of these affordances are used, *self-regulation*, and external assistance does not seem necessary. On the contrary, the members of the community turn to each other, *other-regulation*, to seek answers to their questions about how the affordances work in different ways. In the Survival mode, the children must search for resources, craft items and can gain levels. Furthermore, some resources are connected to the server, the children can control them and they know how to use them, *self-regulation*. One of the children explains a command that is used in one of the play sessions: typing, for example, '/OP+ the name of the player' enables you to use other commands. In the knowledge-making dialogues, it becomes clear that the players can have different kinds of resources, *object-regulation*, although they play together in the same game world. The use of these resources, *object-regulation,* leads to discussions and argumentation among the players. There are knowledge-making dialogues that concern discussions and negotiations about cheating, for example.

One of the children informed the researchers that all the recorded play sessions in this study are published on YouTube® and they all start with an open invitation and instructions as to what people should do if they want to join. YouTube®, *object-regulation/other-regulation*, is an open resource for gaining and sharing knowledge. It is clear that the players do not only address the other players within the community while playing, they also address an assumed audience on YouTube®. As shown in Excerpt 5, this kind of knowledge-making dialogue is an example of cross-pollination

(MacCallum-Stewart 2013), in which the players take an active part in the game and then demonstrate it to others, a relatively new phenomenon (MacCallum-Stewart 2013): *Excerpt 5.*

Player 2:	Kolla nu
	Look now
Player 1:	Va
	What
Player 2:	Nu åkte allting ner
	Now everything went down
Player 1:	Vad ska jag kolla
	What do you want me to look at
Player 2:	Nej jag pratar inte med dig … jag pratar med..
Player 2:	No I'm not talking to you … I'm talking to …

The community contributes to the collective enterprise (Thorne 2012) on YouTube® through their knowledge-making dialogues. This shows how players take an active role in the development and dissemination of Minecraft® and at the same time allow other players to refine, augment and transform their craft (Cayari 2011). The players' commitment to the game leads them to engage in knowledge-making activities outside the game world, in this case to watch recorded play session on YouTube®. The children in the community also share knowledge, which they gained from YouTube®. It has been argued that there are two purposes for children sharing video clips (Ito et al. 2009) and these purposes were both addressed in the children's knowledge-making dialogues in this study. The first is that they want other children to learn and improve their craft and the second is that they want to gain recognition and reputation and reach an audience for their creative work.

Discussion

The aim of this article was to address how online tools and digital technologies can influence data collection opportunities. The following questions were of interest: How can FRAPS® be used to collect data when researching children's knowledge-making dialogues? How can the resources the children use when they collaboratively play Minecraft® be captured?

By using FRAPS® and this methodological approach for data collection, researchers can probably get closer to children's subjective realities by capturing their knowledge-making dialogues while playing Minecraft® in a home setting. In order to fully understand the lifeworlds of children, researchers today must turn to a variety of settings; home, online and together with children. This is in line with Walford (2008b) who claims that an ethnographer does not seek the unusual, rather writes about the routine daily lives of people. Since one of the children in the study already knew how to use FRAPS® none of the researchers needed to be present. In line with, Heath, Hindmarsh, and Luff (2011) who argue that a researcher needs to reflect upon how data collection might alter the behaviour of the participants. All the participants knew that their dialogues were going to be captured and analysed. However, the analytical process of watching all the material several times showed that the children's participation in the study gave the impression that they were not disturbed by the screen captures. It is possible also that the fact that the children were the ones who decided which captures to share and which not to share can have contributed to less interference.

In relation to this, one issue to raise is to what extent children of today are aware of what they actually share and upload on YouTube. Not only what happens on the screen can be shared with an online audience, but also all the dialogues can become wide open for anyone to listen to.

FRAPS® also captured all the disruptions in the communication due to technology problems in real time, as well as the children's immediate reactions to those. Digital tools and artefacts, *object-regulation*, such as computers, headsets, Skype and smart-phones are resources of importance when they collaboratively play together. Excerpt 1 is one example of how they are trying to avoid problems due to technology. This kind of data might have been left out if interviews as a data collection method had been used, as well as Excerpt 2, which shows how they constantly share their experiences while gaming. Furthermore, the meta-conversation, in Excerpt 3, would probably have been very difficult to capture in an interview. However, there are always issues concerning ethics when it comes to including children in research. Swedish researchers have to depart from the guidelines from the Swedish Research Council (2011). From an ethical point of view, this method with using FRAPS® gave all the participating children in the study the opportunity to decide upon which data they wanted to share. This assumption put the researchers involved in this study into the test if they actually could live ethical dilemmas throughout the research process (Mortari and Harcourt 2012; Phelan and Kinsella 2013). By using themselves as ethical tools in the research study, a decision was made to respect the children's decision and avoid asking any further about the play sessions the children did not decide to share.

Turning to the second research question, how can the resources the children use when they collaboratively play Minecraft® be captured, the results from the captured knowledge-making dialogues first show that language is a resource when the children collaboratively play, *other-regulation*, Minecraft® online. Through language use, the players gain and share knowledge since the community gains when the players improve their collaborative skills. Excerpt 1 is an example of the ZPD (Vygotsky 1986), that is what an individual can accomplish in a joint activity when provided with assistance by someone more knowledgeable. Second, the children's previous knowledge and experiences from their ordinary lifeworld can be regarded as resources, which are used in the game. Player 1 is building the roof of the house, as seen in Excerpt 4. Finally, the resources can also be built into the game and their affordances utilized. The players take an active part in the game and then demonstrate it to others online, a relatively new phenomenon (MacCallum-Stewart 2013) as shown in Excerpt 5. To conclude, the results show that the players do not only address the other players within the community while playing, they also address an assumed audience on YouTube®. The children create, spread and share knowledge, which eventually becomes part of a collective enterprise.

Criticism can be raised concerning the fieldwork in this study. If a relatively small amount of time is spent in the field, this might lead us to misunderstand what commonly happens there. On the other hand, the children in the study, the online community, can be considered to be part of a wider focal community, which is in line with Kozinets (2010) who states that through the study of the online community, something significant can be learnt about the wider focal community, their behaviour, its participants and their values or beliefs. To sum up, today, this ought also to work the other way around since the wider focal community easily can be found on YouTube®. Six months of online fieldwork that included watching a variety of clips on YouTube®

contributed to our finding that something significant could be learnt about the online community. There is a huge variety regarding the clips that are uploaded; some people want to show their creative constructions in the most amazing themes, that is, *Star Wars*, *Lord of the Rings*. Meanwhile, other players want to share play sessions while gaming usually providing a secondary narrative over the original one; their walkthrough commentary explains what and how they are doing things. Turning to one of the most interesting results in this study is that YouTube® is used as a resource by the children to collaboratively play Minecraft. Moreover, in particular if the community does not know how to do something, it seems as if the answer always can be found on YouTube®.

Conclusion

The concepts *object-regulation, other-regulation* and *self-regulation* were used to analyse human activities to regulate thinking (Thorne 2012; Thorne, Black, and Sykes 2009) and the model with these concepts was used for analysing the online gaming community. Drawing on Thorne's (2012) model, the single player plays Minecraft and receives feedback from the community and improves his/her knowledge in gaming. Single players and/or a community publish their play sessions on YouTube® and contribute to the collective enterprise which enables single players to seek more knowledge by watching clips and improve their gaming (Golub 2010; Ito et al. 2009). A problem arose when it came to understanding YouTube®, as one of the three categories of regulation, which according to the results in this case study can be regarded as *object-regulation* since it is a cultural artefact. At the same time, this can be understood as *other-regulation* since the uploaded play sessions contain supportive comments and guidance from a more knowledgeable person, acting within a ZPD. This issue needs to be further addressed in future research.

Another issue to address more in depth is whether the method applied in this study can be regarded as virtual ethnography or not. According to Hammersley (2006), virtual ethnography implies that data are collected online without meeting the people face to face. The underlying assumption here is without knowing who the people are. In this case study, all the participants were known to the researchers who were aware that they were all under age; therefore, a letter of consent was needed in line with the Swedish Research Council (2011). Other ethical issues concern, as already mentioned, the wider focal community which can easily be accessed on YouTube®. Data could have been collected, just by using existing uploaded play sessions. This is indeed a question of importance for future researchers to face, assuming that they will use themselves as ethical tools (Mortari and Harcourt 2012) and live ethical dilemmas while researching children's interactions and communications while engaged in gaming (Mortari and Harcourt 2012; Phelan and Kinsella 2013).

However, there are other issues of importance concerning the understanding of online gaming communities, addressed by MacCallum-Stewart (2013) who states that player activity is developing so fast that cohesive studies are very difficult to gather. Moreover, gamers produce new texts with rapidity, which is hard to follow for researchers and the consequence is that there is a lack of research in this area. The ability to collaborate on information sharing and creation has never been greater. Players' experiences can be shared more directly than ever before; as a consequence, the material is easily accessible to everyone.

To conclude, in order for researchers to try to keep up and capture what is going on in online gaming communities, researchers might need to use a diverse series of tools and methods. This case study addresses how online tools and digital technologies can influence data collection opportunities and lead to a greater understanding and deeper involvement in the lives of children playing Minecraft®. Further studies need to be carried out in this area, on how YouTube® can be understood as a resource of great importance for the online gaming community. To sum up, gaming has become such a complex cultural activity that we face numerous possibilities for the study of this field. An interesting question for the future is: How can researchers find ways to conduct studies in order to keep up the pace with the changing face of gaming culture? Is it even possible?

Disclosure statement

No potential conflict of interest was reported by the authors.

Notes

1. FRAPS is a Real-time Video Capture Software that enables players to record their play sessions while gaming www.fraps.com.
2. Vetenskapsrådet.

References

Adler, P. A., and P. Adler. 1996. "Parent-as-Researcher: The Politics of Researching in the Personal Life." *Qualitative Sociology* 19: 35–58.

Bennerstedt, U. 2013. "Knowledge at Play. Studies of Games as Members' Matters." PhD diss., Acta Universitatis Gothoburgensis.

Brandtzaeg, P. B., T. Endestad, J. Heim, B. Hertzberg Kaare, and L. Torgersen. 2004. "Barn i ett digitalt samfunn: En beskrivelse av norske barn fra 7 til 12 år og deras tilgang ti log bruk av TV, PC, Internett, mobiltelefon og spillteknologier." *Barn* 4: 9–31.

Brandtzaeg, P. B., and B. H. Stav. 2004. "Barn og unges skravling på nettet. Social stotte i cyberspace?" *Tidskrift for ungdomsforskning* 4: 27–47.

Buckingham, D. 2006. "Is There a Digital Generation?" In *Digital Generations: Children, Young People and New Media*, edited by D. Buckingham and R. Willett, 1–13. Mahwah, NJ: Erlbaum.

Canossa, A., J. B. Martinez, and J. Togelius. 2013. "Give Me a Reason to Dig Minecraft and Psychology of Motivation." Paper presented at Computational Intelligence in Games (CIG), IEEE, Niagara Falls, ON, August 11–13.

Cayari, C. 2011. "The YouTube Effect: How YouTube Has Provided New Ways to Consume, Create and Share Music." *International Journal of Education and the Arts* 12 (6): 2–29.

Cheng, X., J. Liu, and C. Dale. 2013. "Understanding the Characteristics of Internet Short Video Sharing: A YouTube-Based Measurement Study." *IEEE Transactions of Multimedia* 15 (5): 1184–1194. doi:10.1109/TMM.2013.2265531.

Cohen, C., L. Manion, and K. Morrison,. 2009. *Research Methods in Education*. London: Routledge.

Coppock, V. 2011. "Children as Peer Researchers: Reflections on a Journey of Mututal Discovery." *Children and Society* 25: 435–446. doi:10.1111/j.1099-0860.2010.00296.x.

Golub, A. 2010. "Being in the World (of Warcraft): Raiding, Realism, and Knowledge Production in A Massively Multiplayer Online Game." *Anthropological Quarterly* 83 (1): 17–46.

Grover, S. 2004. "Why Won't They Listen to Us? On Giving Power and Voice to Children Participating in Social Research." *Childhood* 11 (1): 81–93. doi:10.1177/0907568 204040186.

Guimaraes, M. 2005. "Doing Anthropology in Cyberspace: Fieldwork Boundaries and Social Environments." In *Virtual Methods*, edited by C. Hine, 141–156. Oxford: Berg.

Hammersley, M. 2006. "Ethnography: Problems and Prospects." *Ethnography and Education* 1 (1): 3–14. doi:10.1080/17457820500512697.

Heath, C., J. Hindmarsch, and P. Luff. 2011. *Video in Qualitative Research*. London: Sage.

Hine, C. 2005. "Virtual Methods and the Sociology of Cyber-Social-Scientific Knowledge." In *Virtual Methods*, edited by C. Hine, 1–17. Oxford: Berg.

Ito, M., H. Horst, M. Bittanti, D. Boyd, B. Herr-Stephenson, P. G. Lange, C. J. Pascoe, and L. Robinson. 2009. *Living and Learning with New Media: Summary of Findings from the Digital Youth Project*. London: The MIT Press.

Kozinets, R. V. 2010. *Netnography. Doing Ethnographic Research Online*. Croydon: Sage.

Lange, P. G. 2008. "Publicly Private and Privately Public: Social Networking on YouTube." *Journal of Computer-Mediated Communication* 13: 361–380. doi:10.1111/j.1083-6101. 2007.00400.x.

Leavitt, A. 2011. "The Hidden Value of Punching Trees – What *Minecraft* Reveals about Gaming Culture." PAX Prime' 11 (Proceedings), Seattle, WA, August 30–September 12. Accessed May 25, 2014. http://www.g4tv.com/thefeed/blog/post/711028/pax-east-panel-the-hidden-value-of-punching-trees-what-minecraft-teaches-us-about-gamer-culture/.

Lindahl, M., and A.-M. Folkesson. 2012. "Can We Let Computers Change Practice? Educators' Interpretations of Preschool Tradition." *Computers in Human Behavior* 8: 1728–1737. doi:10.1016/j.chb.2012.04.012.

Linderoth, J., S. Björk, and C. Olsson. 2014. "Should I Stay or Should I Go Boundary Maintaining Mechanisms in Left 4 Dead 2." *Authors and Digital Games Research Association DiGRA* 2 (1): 117–145.

MacCallum-Stewart, E. 2013. "Diggy Holes and Jaffa Cakes: The Rise of the Elite Fan-Producer in Video-Gaming Culture." *Journal of Gaming and Virtual Worlds* 5 (2): 165–182. doi:10. 1386/jgvw.5.2.165_1.

Mackay, H. 2005. "New Connections, Familiar Settings: Issues in the Ethnographic Study of New Media Use at Home." In *Virtual Methods*, edited by C. Hine, 129–141. Oxford: Berg.

Markham, A., and N. Baym. 2009. "Making Smart Choices on Shifting Ground." In *Internet Inquiry*, edited by A. Markham and N. Baym, vii–xix. Thousand Oaks, CA: Sage.

Miller, D., and H. A. Horst. 2012. "The Digital and the Human: A Prospectus for Digital Anthropology." In *Digital Anthropology*, edited by H. A. Horst and D. Miller, 3–39. London: Bloomsbury.

Mortari, L., and D. Harcourt. 2012. "'Living' Ethical Dilemmas for Researchers When Researching with Children." *International Journal of Early Years Education* 20 (3): 234–243. doi:10.1080/09669760.2012.715409.

Nutbrown, C. 2010. "Naked by the Pool? Blurring the Image? Ethical Issues in the Portrayal of Young Children in Arts-Based Educational Research." *Qualitative Inquiry* 19: 3–14.

Phelan, S. K., and E. A. Kinsella. 2013. "Picture This . . . Safety, Dignity, and Voice-Ethical Research with Children: Practical Considerations for the Reflexive Researcher." *Qualitative Inquiry* 19 (2): 81–90. doi:10.1177/1077800412462987.

Selwyn, N. 2009. "The Digital Native – Myth and Reality." *Aslib Proceedings: New Information Perspectives* 6: 364–379.

Sveningsson Elm, M. 2009. "How Do Various Notions of Privacy Influence Decisions in Qualitative Internet Research?" In *Internet Inquiry*, edited by A. Markham and N. Baym, 69–88. Thousand Oaks, CA: Sage.

Swedish Research Council. 2011. *Good Research Practice*. Stockholm: Vetenskapsrådet.

Takahasi, T. 2010. "MySpace or Mixi? Japanese Engagement with SNS (Social Networking Sites) in the Global Age." *New Media and Society* 12: 453–475. doi:10.1177/ 1461444809343462.

Thorne, S. L. 2012. "Gaming Writing: Supervernaculars, Stylization, and Semiotic Remediation." In *Technology Across Writing Contexts and Tasks*, edited by G. Kessler, A. Oskoz, and I. Elola, 297–316. San Marcos, TX: CALICO Monograph.

Thorne, S. L., R. W. Black, and J. M. Sykes. 2009. "Second Language Use, Socialization, and Learning in Internet Interest Communities and Online Gaming." *The Modern Language Journal* 93: 802–821.

Thorne, S. L., I. Fischer, and X. Lu. 2012. "The Semiotic Ecology and Linguistic Complexity of an Online Game World." *ReCALL Journal* 24: 243–256. doi:10.1017/S0958344012000158.

Thorne, S. L., and T. Tasker. 2011. "Sociocultural and Cultural-Historical Theories of Language Development." In *Routledge Handbook of Applied Linguistics*, edited by J. Simpson, 487–500. New York: Routledge.

Turkle, S. 2011. *Alone Together. Why We Expect More from Technology and Less from Each Other*. New York: Basic Books.

UN (United Nations). 1989. *The United Nations Convention on the Rights of the Child*. New York: UNICEF.

Vygotsky, L. 1986. *Thought and Language*. Cambridge: MIT Press.

Walford, G. 2008a. "The Nature of Educational Ethnography." In *How to Do Educational Ethnography*, edited by G. Walford, 1–16. London: The Tufnell Press.

Walford, G. 2008b. "Selecting Sites, Gaining Ethical and Practical Access." In *How to Do Educational Ethnography*, edited by G. Walford, 16–39. London: The Tufnell Press.

Wartella, E. A., and N. Jennings. 2010. "Children and Computers: New Technology. Old Concerns." *Princetown University: The Future of Children* 10: 31–43.

Digital stories as a method for evidence-based practice and knowledge co-creation in technology-enhanced learning for children with autism

Sarah Parsons[a], Karen Guldberg[b], Kaśka Porayska-Pomsta[c] and Rachael Lee[d]

[a]Southampton Education School, University of Southampton, Highfield, Southampton SO17 1BJ, UK; [b]School of Education, University of Birmingham, Edgbaston, Birmingham B15 2TT, UK; [c]London Knowledge Lab, Institute of Education, 29 Emerald Street, London WC1N 3QS, UK; [d]Sussex Community NHS Trust, Speech and Language Therapy Service, Unit 3 The Quadrant, 60 Marlborough Road, Lancing, West Sussex BN15 8UW, UK

Storytelling is a powerful means of expression especially for voices that may be difficult to hear or represent in typical ways. This paper reports and reflects on our experiences of co-creating digital stories with school practitioners in a project focusing on embedding innovative technologies for children on the autism spectrum in classroom practice. The digital stories were short films or narrated sequences of slides and images that conveyed key views about experiences and practices with or around the technologies. The creation of the digital stories aimed to empower schools and individual teachers to construct and share their own authentic narratives and to build case examples of creative technology-enhanced teaching and learning. Through focusing on our experiences with one of the schools, we examine the use of digital stories as a method for enabling knowledge co-creation with practitioners and we discuss the evidential potential of digital stories. We argue that the co-creation of digital stories enabled teachers to find their voice in critiquing the usability, usefulness, efficacy and flexibility of the technologies. Furthermore, the stories, both the process of their creation and the final artefacts, provided a concrete grounding for knowledge co-creation about teaching practices and authentic technology-enhanced learning.

Introduction

It is well established that there is a significant gap between research evidence and real-world teaching experiences and practice (Hargreaves 2007; Menter et al. 2010). Many commentators offer both potential solutions for narrowing this gap (Christie and Menter 2009; Hill and Haigh 2012) and critical perspectives on the very concept of evidence-based practice (EBP) in education (Thomas and Pring 2004; Hammersley 2005; Biesta

2007). The recent BERA-RSA (2014) inquiry into EBP noted the importance of teachers' direct involvement in research such ' . . . that wherever possible teachers are active agents in research, rather than passive participants' (8). Crucially, the report concludes:

> . . . that amongst policymakers and practitioners there is considerable potential for greater dialogue than currently takes place, as there is between teachers, teacher-researchers and the wider research community. (8)

This stance is in contrast to other commentaries and policy initiatives from the government, which urge teachers to maximize pupil learning outcomes by focusing on 'what works' via certain teaching methods (cf. Goswami 2006; Thomas 2013). Biesta, Allan, and Edwards (2014) critique this rhetoric, whereby the basic assumptions about what constitutes valid research have been arrogated by the natural sciences' emphasis on gold standard experimental research designs. Consequently, instead of acknowledging the need to employ varying methodologies relating to research foci and diverse contexts, only technical instrumental research appears to be accepted as valid.

The research–practice gap has also been discussed widely in educational and therapeutic autism interventions research (Odom et al. 2005; Dingfelder and Mandell 2011); a field traditionally dominated by methodologies from experimental Psychology, with many studies being undertaken in laboratory settings rather than in classrooms (Parsons et al. 2013). There has been recognition of the paucity of research related to implementation of autism interventions in school settings and of the need for such research (Parsons and Kasari 2013), particularly to improve ecological validity and to generate evidence of long-term effectiveness (Kasari and Smith 2013). Given that the knowledge base of practitioners and the social setting in which practitioners exist are crucial to whether an intervention is applied effectively (Damschroder, Aron, and Keith 2009), the need to bridge the gap between research and educational practice becomes particularly important.

In order to identify the goals that are important for the autism community, for families and for practitioners, it is essential for meaning to be found in all stakeholders' respective lived experiences, and for research to invest in working *with* those stakeholders rather than *on* them (Pellicano, Dinsmore, and Charman 2014). This necessitates a shift of focus from learning that happens outside of the typical places where children spend their time (cf. Ogletree, Oren, and Fischer 2007) to the context and culture of where learning takes place (Thomas 2013). To understand education, we need to recognize that people function in material environments that are endowed with cultural meanings (Lemke 1997; Daniels 2001) which leads to a need to examine both the learning processes and the context of implementation. Such a focus calls for close involvement of practitioners and highlights the importance of action research whereby teachers research their own schools or classrooms to reflect on and improve practice and outcomes for learners (Rudduck and Hopkins 1985; Kemmis, McTaggart, and Nixon 2014).

Deriving from the action research tradition is the important aspiration of participatory research involving practitioners and researchers (Christie and Menter 2009; Leibowitz, Ndebele, and Winberg 2014), and of inclusive research that seeks to fundamentally change the power relationships between researchers and those who are traditionally researched (Seale, Nind, and Parsons 2014). Collaboration and dialogue are considered key to such research, where knowledge is understood to be culturally specific and situated, and hence evidence is an outcome of knowledge co-creation (Fisher, Higgins, and Loveless 2006; Houston et al. 2010). However, despite the aspirational rhetoric of action research and inclusive and participatory involvement of teachers in research, much still remains to be understood about how such involvement can be facilitated and managed in practice and how the emerging outcomes can be meaningfully translated into knowledge that is applicable and relevant beyond the settings within which it was generated.

It is in this context that we discuss the role of digital story-making by school practitioners as a method for generating and sharing new knowledge about how to embed innovative technology-enhanced learning (TEL) in school classrooms. Our research uses digital technologies as both the objects of scrutiny and the methodological means for illustrating their use *in situ*, while enabling and empowering teachers to become active agents in the research. We first present the rationale for the research before providing an overview of the Shape project. We then examine and critique the process of story-making as an example of knowledge co-creation in TEL.

Stories as situated knowledge

Storytelling can be a powerful means of expression especially for voices that may be difficult to hear or represent in typical ways. In this journal's recent special issue on inclusive research (Seale, Nind, and Parsons 2014), many of the papers included aspects of storytelling as part of their methodologies (Black-Hawkins and Amrhein 2014; Hall 2014; MacLeod, Lewis, and Robertson 2014), as ways of sharing and creating meaning from diverse perspectives. Digital storytelling is another way of representing individual narratives and comes from the work of Joe Lambert and Dana Atchley in the USA in the 1980s. The main elements that form the structure and content of a digital story are explained, explored and illustrated in more detail in the latest version of the Digital Storytelling Cookbook (Lambert 2010) along with a specific process for developing stories through workshops and particular techniques. The original conception of digital storytelling arose within an arts-based context, as a desire to capture, value and honour the oral traditions of Jewish and African cultures (Lambert 2010). More recently, digital storytelling has been defined by researchers using the method in broad, technically orientated terms, for example:

> ... a technology application that ... allows computer users to become creative storytellers through the traditional processes of selecting a topic, conducting some research, writing a script, and developing an interesting story. This material is then combined with various types of multimedia, including computer-based graphics, recorded audio, computer-generated text, video clips, and music so that it can be played on a computer, uploaded on a web site, or burned on a DVD. (Robin 2008, 222)

And:

> Digital stories are 3- to 5-min visual narratives that synthesize images, video, audio recordings of voice and music, and text to create compelling accounts of experience. (Gubrium 2009, 186)

In his most recent book, Lambert (2013) highlights the power of digital stories being rooted in the fact that they are natural vehicles for understanding and reflection and for creating meaning. Digital stories ensure that everyone feels they are 'somebody';

they give voice, enable agency and a sense of belonging. They are about valuing experiences as they arise in the *here and now* and are about reflecting on, reviewing and articulating what did and did not work. More specifically, Lambert (2010, 3, our emphasis) discusses the personal and individual in the development of the story:

> As you are putting together your raw material for your story, you are also working to build your narrative voice. *Everyone has a unique style of expressing him or herself* that can jump off the page or resonate in a storytelling presentation.

He contrasts the 'narrative voice' with the 'official voice', which is: ' ... the voice of our expository writing class, our essays and term papers, or our formal memos and letters to our professional colleagues' (3). In other words, in the telling of stories it is a different, less formal, 'more organic and natural' (3) voice that we seek to show. Crucially, as part of the natural voice, Lambert (2010) also discusses the importance of emotional content in the stories and how the storyteller should reflect on, and seek to convey, their personal involvement in, and emotional connection with, the story. This aligns with Labov's (1972) narrative features in storytelling which, he argues, have two main functions: (1) a referential function in which the teller gives information by referring to the experience, or by recapitulating it, for example, the reporting what happened; and (2) an evaluative function where the teller communicates the meaning of the narrative by establishing some point of personal involvement, and the speaker's perspective on what it all means. In other words, the stories are developed from personal perspectives and should convey what the storyteller seeks to communicate.

As implied in Robin's (2008) and Gubrium's (2009) definitions, the particular value of the *digital* story compared to other kinds of stories is that the visual is combined with sound and, often (but not always), motion. The advent of Web 2.0 technologies and the ease, with which images, video and sounds can be captured, edited and disseminated, enable personal narratives and experiences to be documented and shared in relatively brief presentations. For example, Gubrium (2009) discusses the use of digital stories as a method in community-based participatory research about women's reproductive health experiences where they offer a grounded way to capture and document experiences that ' ... inserts indigenous empirical material into research endeavors' [*sic*] (186). That is, there is a more direct insight into situated knowledge that can be gained through digital stories by being able to show specific contexts in visual and/or audio form (cf. Harrison, Sengers, and Tatar 2011).

Moreover, the process of creating a digital story can help individuals reflect on and 'own' their experiences and stories, and to receive validation through the story being 'screened' to others (Gubrium 2009, 189). In other words, the *process* of story creation and the production of a tangible artefact as an *outcome* that can be viewed and reflected upon by others are two of the key aspects of digital storytelling (Lambert 2010). These features make digital stories as a research method different from other forms of visual research methods, for example, photo-elicitation (Shohel 2012), stimulated recall (Vesterinen, Toom, and Patrikainen 2010) and video narratives (Taylor et al. 2011). In these examples, images and/or video were used as cues to aid recall and reflection on the specific context or practice example. That is, the videos and pictures are used as tools for prompting verbal responses and discussion in interviews and it is this dialogue that forms the main research data for analysis and dissemination. By contrast, in digital storytelling it is the stories themselves that are the main vehicle for constructing, presenting and disseminating knowledge: they are stand-alone objects that capture and document practice, views and experiences from the perspective(s) of the storyteller(s).

Digital stories have been used widely in community activism, public health care, social services, international development, public broadcasting and in business (Lambert 2013). As a method, they have also been used to engage and empower marginalized young people (Lowenthal 2009). However, only recently has this method been applied in educational contexts (Robin 2008; Ohler 2013) and this has tended to take two main forms: (1) as constructivist teaching and learning activities for students to enhance digital media skills as well as topic-specific learning outcomes through deeper engagement with the material (Ohler 2013) and (2) as a means through which teachers can encourage discussion of topics by presenting information in a way that makes ' ... abstract or conceptual content more understandable' (Robin 2008, 224). We argue that in the Shape project our use and discussion of digital stories as *evidential artefacts in research* is different from these methodological applications in that the Shape stories offer direct and grounded opportunities to capture, document and reflect upon emergent TEL-related practices in schools (cf. Gubrium 2009).

The 'Shape' project: shaping the future of educational technologies today – from prototypes to practice

Project overview

The objectives of the Shape project were to (i) draw upon four multi-disciplinary TEL projects to disseminate and explore creative ways in which children's social communication skills and understanding can be supported in schools and (ii) to create the foundations for the development of an effective online community whereby practitioners and researchers could address how to extend the use of TEL for this group of children. One of the main motivations for the project was to enable us to translate the findings of this research into further development of the technologies and of their applications, to make them more robust to withstand different school settings and real-world usage and to enable technology designs that are able to support teachers in being autonomously creative in their practices. We used a participatory approach where the project team worked with teachers and children in six special, specialist and mainstream schools. In this paper, we focus on digital story creation as a methodology for (i) identifying how teachers were using the technologies and (ii) disseminating their practice in using the technologies. We draw specifically on our experiences with one of the autism specialist schools – Radlett Lodge – and the paper is co-written with the school's lead Speech and Language specialist. Two main technology-based prototypes from previously funded TEL projects were used in the Shape project – ECHOES and COSPATIAL – and these are briefly described next before an explanation of how we developed the digital stories is given.

ECHOES was funded jointly by the Economic and Social Research Council (ESRC) and Engineering and Physical Sciences Research Council under the TLRP (teaching and learning research programme)-TEL (technology-enhanced learning) programme in the UK and had the aim to support typically developing children and children on the autism spectrum to explore, rehearse and acquire skills that are fundamental to social interaction, such as turn-taking, the ability to engage in joint activities with others and in reciprocal interactions. The ECHOES prototype is set in a 'magic garden', which is populated with a semi-autonomous virtual character and interactive

Figure 1.   A child playing with ECHOES on a big multi-touch screen.

objects that are used as triggers for engaging the child in an interaction (with or without the virtual character). For example, the child might take turns with the virtual character to grow flowers by shaking a rain cloud or to stack flowerpots to build a tower out of them. The virtual character will encourage and support the child in completing the activity. The interactivity is therefore organized around discrete activities, each with a pre-defined pedagogic purpose relating to turn-taking skills, sharing attention with others as well as initiating and responding to bids for interaction. In the Shape project, ECHOES was used in dedicated spaces in schools and was presented on a large multi-touch screen, with the interactions between the technology and the children being facilitated through touch (see Figure 1).

COSPATIAL (Communication and Social Participation: Collaborative Technologies for Interaction And Learning) was funded by the European Commission's FP7 programme. The project's main aim was to develop and apply collaborative technologies to promote learning and understanding of collaboration and social conversation for children on the autism spectrum. Prototypes were designed with the close involvement of teachers and children (with and without autism) in both mainstream and special schools (Parsons et al. 2011; Parsons and Cobb 2014). The Shape project involved the

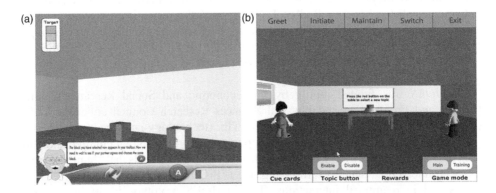

Figure 2.   Screen shots from COSPATIAL's Block Challenge (left) and Talk2U (right).

COSPATIAL Collaborative Virtual Environments (CVEs) 'Block Challenge' and 'Talk2U' (see Figure 2). Block Challenge is a two-player game focusing on collaboration, turn-taking and perspective taking in which children have to co-operate and communicate to stack dual-coloured virtual blocks in a pattern that matches a target; each child has a different target and only specific blocks, oriented in a particular way, meet the target pattern. Talk2U focuses on social conversation and provides a structured, prompted framework in which children can practice different elements of social conversation (e.g. starting, maintaining, switching topic and ending) before engaging in a social conversation with the other player; both players, plus a teacher who facilitates and supports the conversation, are represented in the CVE as virtual characters, and rewards (virtual stars) are given by the teacher for good effort and performance.

Methodology

Development of the ingredients for the digital stories

We began the process of digital storytelling by running a series of half- or full-day workshops at the schools involved, first introducing narrative concepts, before covering more technical issues such as camera work, sound and editing. The workshops generated a great deal of discussion, and to some extent caused concern that the project would become onerous if the expertise in storytelling was perceived to be missing. Some members of teaching staff were unsure initially because they did not understand the term 'digital stories' and so this was perceived as a jargon phrase that felt somewhat alienating and complicated. However, we demonstrated practical methods for explaining how humans are natural storytellers and most of the teaching staff quickly grasped that this is something that they already do, particularly in relation to concepts already familiar in the Key Stages 1 and 2 curricula, such as the 'story mountain'. The story mountain builds from an opening through an event, or sequence of events, that present a problem, question or big event, before showing a solution (or resolution) and then an ending. The workshop then adopted the story mountain as a structure for helping staff develop example stories based on their experiences in the classroom. This emphasizes the need for researchers and practitioners to find a common language in order to be able to work together in a way that is comfortable, respectful and which enables both sides to cross boundaries (Rynes, Bartunek, and Daft 2001). The use of the 'story mountain' meant that we were using a concept that teachers were familiar with using, and therefore, demystifying the process of creating narrative through digital story creation.

Even though we ran workshops in the capturing and editing process, many teachers were already using digital cameras, phones and iPads. Nevertheless, the time available for capturing and creating stories was a concern raised by the teachers. We placed an emphasis on the stories being led by the school personnel, but which were co-created with the help of the research team; in other words, the creation of the digital stories was focused on the stories that schools wanted to tell and the experiences they wanted to share. We were very clear that the focus could be critical as well as positive and that we were interested in a range of experiences and views. We were also very clear that the focus of the project was not about taking a narrow view on 'effectiveness', that is, only concerned with whether the use of the technologies were supporting particular learning outcomes for children (as would be the focus in a more traditional research approach), but rather about the school's experiences with the technologies in a much wider sense, including any challenges faced in implementing the technologies within the context of everyday school life.

ECHOES and COSPATIAL were left with school to explore and use as they wished, with the children they identified as potentially benefitting from their use. The research team provided some initial information about what the technologies had been designed to do and how they had been used previously, but made no other stipulations about when, where, for how long, in what ways and with whom the technologies should be used. Nevertheless, the use of prototype technologies, not yet commercially available and developed in previous projects by research team members, provided the *starting point* for the co-construction of knowledge within this project. That is, ECHOES and COSPATIAL represented the research team's initial contributions to knowledge that was shared with the school. The school was asked to work with these specific technologies in order to contribute their knowledge and experiences about where and how the technologies could be used in their lessons and classrooms. These processes, along with the perceived outcomes for the school, provided the focus for joint reflection between the teachers and the researchers, and for the co-creation of the digital stories (see the next section).

The school was provided with digital video cameras to record interactions of the children and staff with the project technologies as well as any reflections or perspectives on their experiences. The school worked with the technologies over a period of about four months, implementing their use during the school day and capturing this via video, with limited involvement from the research team. Seven children with autism, aged from 6 to 15 years, and around 10 members of staff were involved in the activities captured on video, but it was the Speech and Language Therapist (co-author, Rachael Lee) who was the driver of the project within the school. With the full backing of the senior management team of the school, she timetabled and organized lessons using the technologies, ensuring that sessions were videoed and that staff, and students (where possible), provided feedback and reflection on their experiences. This was managed explicitly for some teaching staff in the form of direct interviews to camera (with questions being asked by Rachael), and also more implicitly for students, for example, through designing one of the lessons as a 'focus group' so that feedback on views and experiences could be gathered (see 'Working Party' in Table 1). As well as filming lessons that involved the use of ECHOES and COSPATIAL by the students, 'staging' or potential 'cut-away' shots were also filmed and photographed, including the set-up of the technologies and the room(s) in which they would be used and images showing additional materials that teachers developed to support the lessons. These are good examples of where the capturing of material for the videos went beyond a straight forward exposition of 'what happened'; that is, video materials were planned, scripted and filmed so that they could be used as parts of a story that could be edited together.

Co-creation of the digital stories

In total, approximately 10 hours of video footage was taken over the four-month period. Having planned and collected the videos and photographs, the school personnel did not feel that they had the time or expertise to edit clips to form their stories and so chose to involve the project team in bringing the digital stories to fruition. Two members of the project team met with Rachael for a full day to watch some of the footage and discuss the stories that the school identified as wanting to be told. Crucially, it was Rachael who

Table 1. Summary of the four digital stories from Radlett Lodge with hyperlinks to the stories.

Story title with hyperlink	Participants	Main technology used	Story summary
Collaboration by stealth (see https://www.youtube.com/watch?feature=player_embedded&v=dMC63lMZNSk)	David (15), Ahmed (14) and Ciaran (13); Rachael (Speech and Language Therapist); Stephen (Teacher); Mary (Learning Support Assistant)	COSPATIAL	Presents how they worked on maintaining and exiting conversations appropriately. The boys were all very motivated by using the software and COSPATIAL gave them a way to work on these aspects in a novel manner. They have historically found learning social conversation skills difficult, hence the emphasis on 'learning by stealth' i.e. focusing on a challenging task without realizing they are learning!
Outside the box (see https://www.youtube.com/watch?feature=player_embedded&v=ApVITUeeBFI)	As above	COSPATIAL	Presents how COSPATIAL became more than just a teaching tool and intervention but it also helped with assessment procedures. The technology supported the staff to become more aware of how to break down conversations into specific parts. It also helped staff identify the specific difficulties the boys had with conversation skills. In addition, pairs of students worked together and got out of their comfort zones in the process. These pairings had unexpected gains as it helped the staff think 'outside the box' about how to support the students

(Continued)

Table 1. (Continued).

Story title with hyperlink	Participants	Main technology used	Story summary
Working party (see https://www.youtube.com/watch?feature=player_embedded&v=mX_UnysuTSs)	As above	COSPATIAL	Presents the process of a focus group activity that Rachael conducted with the boys to feedback on their experiences and their thoughts about the software. The boys then watched themselves talking about, and using, the software. It was clear that the work with COSPATIAL enabled them to improve their communication skills with one another and to gain confidence. In this clip, the students also make suggestions about how to improve the technology
Playing with ECHOES (see https://www.youtube.com/watch?feature=player_embedded&v=2ZvSjbWz72I)	Hammad (7), Sabir (6), Aaron (9), Shivam (9) and various members of staff from Radlett Lodge School	ECHOES	Presents the way in which teachers used ECHOES with the individual children. ECHOES was used to engage in activities in collaboration with the child and to prompt them to act in particular ways. Teachers also used ECHOES to 'sabotage' some children's actions to see how they react and this has often provoked behaviours from the children that would provide teachers with a view on what the individual children may be capable of. Access to such children's capabilities is important in allowing the teachers to tailor the individual interventions appropriately

came with clear ideas about the main stories she – on behalf of colleagues and students – wanted to tell. Therefore, the stories from this school were very much driven by them and by the experiences of the different staff and children taking part. We first discussed the key messages that Rachael wanted to convey from the schools' experiences; for COSPATIAL there were three: (1) the use of COSPATIAL fired the children's imagination, (2) encouraged teamwork and (3) the technology is a tool not a teacher – support and good teaching are needed. For ECHOES, which in contrast with COSPATIAL, was used by a younger (4–6 years old) and predominantly non-verbal group of children, the key message also related to the technology as an enhancement of the existing practices rather than a replacement for the teachers. Specifically, teachers' observations related to the fact that ECHOES allowed them (1) to tailor their own interaction with the individual children, using the technology as a pre-text for collaboration, turn-taking and eliciting spontaneous responses from the children, for example, when the teachers sabotaged a routine activity such as bubble popping by turning it into a game between the teacher and the child, and (2) to gain insight into individual children's abilities, for example, their ability to focus on some aspects of the environment, which would have been difficult to observe in routine classroom environment.

We then watched together some of the video footage to identify particularly pertinent clips that could be used to illustrate the key messages and talked about how we could start to construct stories that showed these messages clearly. Having been present at all of the videoed sessions, and having a vision for the stories that she and the teachers at the school wanted to tell, Rachael was able to point us towards particular sessions with staff and students that showed interesting and relevant interactions and comments. This led to an initial drafting of the core elements of the stories by the project team members. For example, developing the idea about how COSPATIAL fired the children's imagination, we generated the following brief:

> This is a story that should emphasise the motivation, excitement, joy and focus that was observed in the sessions when the boys were working with COSPATIAL. There is a sense of exploration and freedom about some of the activity that was experienced very positively; as Rachael said: 'they were doing something that they did not want to do without realising it!' Include: clips of the boys working on COSPATIAL with Rachael to show: motivation, focus, excitement, exploration, and communication, via the co-construction/selection/creation of characters' attributes. Link these with something from Steven about the benefits and Rachael's prompting question about this. Could be structured around different stages: setting-up; finding out what's there; exploring? Note that Mary says 'these two don't really [normally] speak to each other'.

Working with this brief, one of the research team members then spent a further day independently collating and sequencing clips to build the story. This created a storyboard (one that listed in sequence the clips to be used rather than showing images), which was then shared with Rachael for checking. In this way, the stories were negotiated and ultimately co-created through the project team interpreting, from shared discussions and joint viewing of clips, how the story could be told. In other words, it was the responsibility of the project team to bring the school's anticipated stories to life.

Rachael was happy with the storyboards and also said that she could provide a voice-over for any of the stories if needed. The storyboards showing the timing, and start and end points, of each clip were then sent to a member of the project team who took responsibility for editing. The editing process for each digital story took approximately 48 hours. The draft-edited digital stories were then shared with

Rachael for initial approval, before being shared with the pupils, their parents and the staff for their agreement that the stories could be made public on the project website. Permissions and approvals were given and everyone felt happy with the stories without the need for voice-overs or the addition of music; it was felt strongly that the stories, emphasizing experiences and voices, were clear without the need for further embellishment or explanation. As Rachael explains:

> We all absolutely loved them [the stories]! The parents were also all really pleased with the outcomes and a couple of parents viewed the stories with their son as well which prompted a lot of interesting discussions! The video clips were fantastic and so well selected from a huge mass of film to back up the relevant points in a succinct and clear story.

Eventually, four stories of 22 minutes in total (around five minutes each) were created from the hours of video footage taken at Radlett Lodge (overall, the project created 27 digital stories with the six different school communities); the story brief included earlier became 'Collaboration by Stealth'. A summary of the stories is included in Table 1, which also provides hyperlinks to each story so that the digital stories form an integral part of this dissemination.

Analysis and conceptualization of the videos as digital stories, and digital stories as evidence

Space constraints preclude us from presenting and analysing each of the Radlett Lodge stories in detail, but we include one of the stories here for more explicit scrutiny and evaluation in relation to features of storytelling as distinct from narrative. Specifically, by using the teachers' concept and understanding of the story mountain, we developed structure in the stories with a clear beginning, middle and an end. A detailed discussion of the conceptual differences between narrative and story is beyond the scope of the present paper but we suggest that individual, digital stories were created in the project which were not simply exposition or narrative; the stories have referential *and* evaluative functions (Labov 1972), including emotional engagement, personal experiences and a natural rather than a formal voice (Lambert 2010). Moreover, Hagel (2013) argues that narratives are open ended and unfinished, while stories are closed ended; by following a story mountain structure our stories reached conclusions and were, *ipso facto*, closed ended. In agreement with Corman (2013), we argue that the Shape project produced, through subsequent analysis and reflection (as here), a 'local narrative' which is a ' . . . system of stories about events in the here-and-now . . . .[they] define a place where individuals can cast themselves in roles, aligning their personal narratives'. In other words, the synthesis that we bring to the stories in this paper is the *local narrative* that reflects the *system of stories* from Radlett Lodge. Table 2 presents a précis of one of the stories – 'Outside of the Box' – mapped to key elements of a story mountain structure; as well as the personal engagement with the story by the storyteller(s) (cf. Lambert 2010).

In addition, Table 2 summarizes a content analysis of the story using Schrum et al.'s (2005, 204) framework for a 'platinum standard' of acceptable evidence in the field of school-based TEL research, comprising: (1) teacher beliefs about technology, (2) teacher practice with technology and (3) student learning outcomes. Schrum and colleagues are editors of scholarly journals dedicated to TEL research, who argue for the reconsideration and improvement of the quality of evidence in the field, placing a particular emphasis on the need for *authentic research*. Authenticity in this respect

Table 2. Example of story analysis for structure, content and personal engagement of 'Outside the Box'.

Clip description	'Story mountain' structure	Storyteller's personal engagement with the story	Story content mapped to Schrum et al.'s (2005) platinum standard for evidence in TEL research (beliefs, practice, outcomes)
The story starts by Rachael talking directly to the camera, describing how the COSPATIAL technology has enabled her to understand more about how to teach conversation skills. She explains how one of the students she worked with was able to learn how to switch conversations and how the technology can support this continued focus	*Opening* – sets the scene about storyteller's own learning through the project and the value of the technologies for the students	We hear how Rachael's knowledge about teaching conversation skills has been enhanced. Rachael's own learning through the project is articulated: 'enabled me … not just for the children but for myself …'	*Practices*: Technology can provide a tool to help with the assessment of difficulties and a particular example is described *Beliefs*: Rachael is surprised about the insights provided through using the technology; her existing beliefs are challenged *Outcomes*: topic-switching in conversations is specifically identified as a challenge for one of the students, and subsequent support provided for them to work on this

(Continued)

Table 2. (Continued).

Clip description	'Story mountain' structure	Storyteller's personal engagement with the story	Story content mapped to Schrum et al.'s (2005) platinum standard for evidence in TEL research (beliefs, practice, outcomes)
The continued focus is illustrated in the next clip which shows David and Ahmed in a room using the software with Rachael's support. The clip shows how she supports the students to learn how to switch topic whilst using the software to support this process. This clip also shows the boys engaging positively in the learning experience and focusing on what is being asked of them. Additional (non-technology-based) materials (pictorial jigs) are also shown being used to support understanding and engagement	Event (initial) – illustrating the specific skills that are being taught using the technologies and which Rachael has found most useful	The story starts to show Rachael taking control of what they were doing at the school and how their own expertise was used in deciding where to go with this work	Practices: scaffolding of student engagement within and around the technology is shown; re-purposing of the technology compared to original intended use Outcomes: positive engagement of students with the technology and each other
The story switches to Mary talking about how it is interesting how pairs of children have worked together, and how these pairings have enabled them to mix with different people and develop their social skills. Mary says that using COSPATIAL has challenged them to go out of their comfort zone and do something a little bit different	Event (build) – raises the idea of the value of thinking differently about the students and how to constructively challenge them: 'you wouldn't have imagined them going out to the playground together, or sitting next to each other in class'	We hear Mary's surprise about the use of COSPATIAL and how the children responded: 'I think it's quite interesting …' 'It's quite fascinating …'	Beliefs: challenging expectations and assumptions about who 'usually' works together, and children's individual skills and abilities. Risk-taking shown in pairing different children to work together Outcomes: positive experiences reported for the students involved

Rachael then talks to camera: she is interested in the students' reactions to Block Challenge. Rachael outlines how it is interesting how one of the students had to get over the initial hurdle of thinking from another person's perspective. Once he had done that, he could apply it. For his next step, she would like to see his next step as increasing the difficulty for him	*Posing the main question* – the extent to which different skills and abilities are revealed or uncovered in the use of COSPATIAL, and how progress can be made by students	Rachael's surprise at how one of the students responded is revealed: 'I was very interested in his reaction . . . to get over that initial hurdle'	*Beliefs*: Rachael's assumed knowledge about an individual student is challenged when the student finds some aspects of the task surprisingly difficult *Practices*: articulating how this new awareness about the student will influence planning for future sessions; illustrating the individualization of approach taken
The story moves to shots of the student using the software and showing how the difficulty was increased for him. It shows the student asking questions of the other student to understand his perspective	*Solution (answering the main question)* – showing how the student is working on the particular skill that is difficult for him, and how progress is being made through using the technology	We see Rachael's personal involvement in supporting the student to work on this challenging aspect. He is shown working constructively with another student on the task: 'Let's figure this out first right . . . ok . . . so here we go . . .'	*Practices*: shows how the technology is being used with and by the students to support their understanding *Outcomes*: demonstrates learning in action and shows that the initial difficulties described by Rachael could be overcome with support
The story ends with excerpts from an interview with Steven, a teacher at the school, where Rachael asks directly whether skills used in COSPATIAL are transferable. Steven says they are absolutely transferable but that this is very dependent on the teacher ensuring that they consider how to transfer the skills outside the technology. Then he talks about how he might work to transfer those skills using the software as a framework but without having the software there	*Ending/conclusions* – looking to the future i.e. further progress is possible through the exploration of similar skills outside of using the technology: '. . . there is plenty of scope for teaching material there which I could use in a much more generalised manner'	We see Rachael interviewing Steven to help her to reflect on the value of the project from the perspective of a professional colleague. The implicit message is that Rachael – as the main storyteller – agrees with the views expressed by Steven. The explicit message is that Steven is very positive about the project and can see how the work so far can be extended: 'It's up to me as to how much they could be questioned . . . and how much we could experiment with the same idea'	*Beliefs*: tacit knowledge between colleagues is made explicit in this exchange; Steven's views about the benefits of COSPATIAL for his students are expressed. Suggests the potential for generalization of skills and understanding *Practices*: ideas are generated for extending the work to support generalization of skills; planning for the future

examines ' ... connections between beliefs, practices and learning outcomes' carried out in the context of real schools and classrooms, and demonstrating evidence of use via (for example) video case studies (Schrum et al. 2005, 206). Thus, our analysis focuses on highlighting the beliefs and practices of teachers, as well as the learning outcomes for students, illustrated in the digital stories.

Findings

Insights into e-inclusion practices

The process of creating the digital stories offered teachers an opportunity not only to revisit and scrutinize the interactions between themselves and the children, and between children and the technology, but also for debating what aspects of those interactions were essential elements for the stories that they wanted to tell. In the use of COSPATIAL and ECHOES, teachers acknowledged their surprise at how children had engaged with the technologies, with some of this only becoming apparent through the creation of the digital stories and the representations of use captured therein. We suggest that, by revealing the beliefs and practices of teachers, as well as the learning outcomes of students (Schrum et al. 2005), the digital stories provided insights into e-inclusion practices, which ' ... emphasizes the interaction between digital tools, contexts and people, and focuses attention on the activity of the use of digital technologies' (Abbott 2007, 6).

Regarding *teachers' beliefs*, the Shape project took the approach that educational practice is more than the application of specific strategies to meet pre-determined ends and it addressed the particular contexts in which problems needed to be tackled. The digital story creation process enhanced practitioners' abilities to interpret and make sense of what they were doing. It contributed to giving them new understandings regarding their practice and helped them see and imagine their practice differently. For example, the speech and language specialist highlighted that the process helped her to reflect more carefully about how she taught communication skills to children with autism. It pushed her to encourage children who did not normally collaborate, to do so. Teachers took risks in their application of the technologies by pairing different children with each other and being creative in how the technologies were used. The process of reviewing the digital stories also provided insights into how children had developed their understandings through the use of the technologies, enabling staff members to engage with the responses of the pupils, to gauge whether the work was making sense to them and to check children's understanding through careful questioning and listening. For some practitioners, viewing and reviewing the digital stories also enabled them to identify new and nuanced information about children (see hyperlinked stories in Table 1).

Moreover, Rachael Lee also reflected on how she, and colleagues at the school, felt that they were able to contribute to knowledge as collaborators in, rather than recipients of, research due to the flexible and approachable ethos of the project:

> It was very refreshing and different to not have to be so constrained by a preordained clinical format and stringent participant selection systems etc ... a flexible approach is crucial and all too often I have seen potentially important research projects fall through due to the amount of constraints stopping our pupils accessing a study. I felt really empowered by the researchers and not just [being] someone carrying out protocols to generate results to be taken away and analysed elsewhere. I feel this has been the most appropriately targeted project I have been involved in.

Such creativity and daring suggests that teachers experienced agency and empowerment in how the technologies were used, and in the creation of the digital stories. Gubrium (2009, 190) notes that 'The digital story process featured the agency of participants in ways a prestructured [*sic*] research agenda could not', and this accords with our experiences too. The knowledge co-creation on which we embarked with the school staff was about respecting their independence and genuine desire to understand their contexts, challenges and ways of using the technologies in their settings, in order to inform further development of the technologies as well as reflection on teaching practices and pupil progress. This is very different from the dominant rhetoric that is focused on critiquing the teaching profession's perceived weaknesses in drawing on EBPs (Biesta 2007). It is also quite different from much of TEL research, which often fails to reach beyond the life-times of specific projects to examine how the technologies developed actually become appropriated by teachers, the extent to which they can be appropriated without researchers' involvement and what, if anything, makes teachers feel at ease with using the technologies in their daily practices.

Regarding *teachers' practices*, the process of knowledge co-creation through the digital stories highlighted key features for making TEL interventions work in schools and revealed new insights about TEL teaching and learning practices. Teachers regularly re-purposed the technologies, scaffolding children's engagement in different ways than intended by the original TEL projects. Specifically, teachers responded to the individual needs of the pupils using their pedagogical content knowledge (Mishra and Koehler 2006). For example, with the COSPATIAL technology, the lead professional utilized pictorial 'jigs' from the structured teaching approaches of TEACCH (Mesibov, Shea, and Schopler 2004), alongside the structure and prompts that had been programmed into the technology. In the ECHOES sessions, teachers encouraged children to interact with the technology by physically supporting their engagement, demonstrating in the process a clear sharing of space and attention. Thus, the affordances of the technologies supported collaboration in different ways, which the teachers explored and extended in their sessions.

The motivation and enjoyment of the pupils in using the technologies highlighted the need for schools to be flexible in when and how the technologies were used. For example, some of the younger children wanted to use the ECHOES environment on days when it was not a part of their timetable. Accommodating this motivation and enjoyment was challenging for the school because space was very limited and the technologies had to be set-up each time they were to be used. Nevertheless, the teachers were willing to support and schedule children's engagement in a flexible way. Flexibility and patience were also required by the schools due to the technical difficulties experienced with the COSPATIAL and ECHOES technologies (both prototypes rather than commercial programmes). This underscores the level of interest and support that is needed by schools to be able to work with new technologies in spaces and contexts that are not tailored for their use, and when the technologies themselves are not yet as robust as they need to be to allow their systematic and independent use by teachers. A school with less patience and vision about how the technologies could be used would very likely have withdrawn or become frustrated with the project quite quickly. Nevertheless, this also highlights what can be done even in less than ideal circumstances when there are enthusiastic and positive staff members who are willing to commit time and effort to the project, with the full support of the school's management team. Indeed, the school leadership was vital in the success of this process; their strength of vision translated into support for staff time and technical assistance.

In terms of *learning outcomes* for the students, one of the main motivating factors for school personnel was seeing the pupils' clear enjoyment when using the technologies and how much they learned with apparent minimal effort. These positive, quality interactions also helped school staff to learn more about the pupils than in previous assessment sessions, as illustrated in the analysis of 'Outside the Box' in Table 2. The children showed their excitement and enthusiasm for using the technologies, through verbal reports and reflections, and also as captured in their verbal and nonverbal responses during the videoed sessions. The teachers, and older students, made design recommendations for improving the technologies; indeed, this session ('Working Party' – see Table 1) is a good example of where the creation of the digital stories facilitated the sharing of critical and constructive feedback, thereby supporting ideas for further development of TEL environments. The staff could see that the project was real and making a clear difference; not least because three of the participating children also had specific targets in their Individual Education Plans (IEPs) relating to social conversation, which they all achieved.

Critical reflections on the process and outcomes

Through the process of digital story creation, we developed a respectful and safe space for all in which different 'ways of knowing' could be produced and shared (Hall 2014). We concur with Hall, who argues that by taking a more radical shift away from conventional research paradigms and towards more dialogic forms of knowledge – via storytelling – the tendency for dominant cultures to impose epistemological assumptions is reduced, thereby allowing indigenous views and experiences to be expressed in more authentic and meaningful ways. Crucially, Hall (2014) emphasizes the value and importance of *stories as evidence* in their own right, rather than simply as a vehicle to support the expression of views in different ways (though this can also be a powerful method). Such a position is also well represented in the wealth of biographical and narrative research that illuminates experiences and perspectives from different groups and individuals (Denzin and Lincoln 2011; Andrews, Squire, and Tamboukou 2013).

Similarly, Grove (2013) makes a case for the structural similarities between the creation of stories and the creation of evidence through research. She argues that both stories and research have directionality that contextualizes, prompts and discusses specific questions or issues. Both stories and research have themes or topics that they focus on – they come from a particular genre (or paradigm) – and are presented in particular ways, usually with a beginning, middle and an end. In addition, both storytelling and research are influenced and/or underpinned by theories, especially theories about the positioning of the storyteller in relation to the audience. For example, in the same way that participants in research are positioned in different ways depending on the underlying epistemological position of the research, so too do storytellers occupy different positions in relation to their audience: as conveyors of information, as sharers of information and as collaborators in the creation of information.

We suggest that there is an equivalence between these positions of the storyteller with the concepts of knowledge transfer, knowledge exchange and knowledge co-creation, respectively. Specifically, *knowledge transfer* suggests a one-way application of knowledge *from* the researchers *to* the practitioners (ESRC, n.d.-a), whilst *knowledge exchange* suggests a more reciprocal relationship *between* researchers and practitioners, namely, 'a two-way process where social scientists and individuals or organisations share learning, ideas and experiences' (ESRC, n.d.-b). However, as also suggested implicitly by the ESRC (n.d.-b), the power and direction of influence in knowledge exchange still lies very much with the researchers rather than the wider stakeholders (our emphasis):

> By creating a dialogue between these communities, knowledge exchange helps *research to influence policy and practice* ... Collaborative activity can lead to a better understanding of the ways in which academic research can add value and offer insights to key issues of concern for policy and practice.

By contrast, we argue that *knowledge co-creation* represents a more innovative attempt to shift away from these traditional conceptions of knowledge transfer and knowledge exchange towards a much more shared (and shareable) endeavour, which is 'genuinely collective' and 'synergistic' (Leibowitz, Ndebele, and Winberg 2014, 3). Such a shift is in line with participatory (or inclusive; Walmsley 2004; Nind 2014) approaches to research which focus:

> ... on a process of sequential reflection and action, carried out with and by local people rather than on them. Local knowledge and perspectives are not only acknowledged but form the basis for research and planning. (Cornwall and Jewkes 1995, 1667)

In a similar way that the voices of indigenous peoples are silenced or re-purposed by dominant cultures (Hall 2014), the prevailing research culture of knowledge transfer in evidence-based teaching diminishes the potential contributions of teachers and children by prioritising particular 'ways of knowing' through positivistic research paradigms (Rynes, Bartunek, and Daft 2001). Such paradigms fail to take into account the situated nature of the experiences and expectations of teachers and children in schools (Parsons et al. 2013), and the complex nature of schools where it is often difficult to implement more rigid, experimental research designs requiring strict adherence to planned protocols (Kasari and Smith 2013). Thus, in the Shape project, we worked with the idea that digital stories could provide a way of placing teachers' and children's worldviews at the centre of the research (cf. Hall 2014) such that schools would be empowered to create and share their own authentic stories and to build case examples of creative teaching and learning. In reflecting on the process for the school, Rachael suggests that this was achieved in the Shape project:

> ... the stories were based on the salient experiences we felt needed to be told and recorded ... [they] were a perfect way to document our experiences. However the best thing about them is that the research results were accessible to parents, professionals and the participants alike – something very few projects can achieve.

The aim of such empowerment is to create a means not only for research and practice to be aware of one another, but crucially, to be mutually informing, co-influencing and co-evolving. This meant finding ways to truly value the craft and personal knowledge of teachers (Thomas and Pring 2004), to take on board their tacit knowledge and skills and to value professional experience as research evidence in its own right. Our focus on the value of what practitioners were doing, rather than focusing on particular ends prescribed by us via a priori research designs, meant that professionals were themselves making judgements about the most appropriate course of action. The process of digital story creation elicited knowledge from practitioners. For example, the video recordings were used to identify key episodes in children's progress and learning and how teachers could offer support. Practitioners could then reflect on how support was selected in the moment, such that meaningful links could be made between observable aspects of a given learning situation, teachers' interpretations of the situation and their subsequent pedagogic decisions. These links, created and presented via the digital stories, provide evidence of e-inclusion practices (Abbott 2007) by making explicit the tacit knowledge and experiences of practitioners and, thus, available for inspection and sharing. In this way, the digital stories show how teachers implementing TEL can respond to learner differences in a way that enables learners to be included in the daily life of the classroom (cf. Black-Hawkins, Florian, and Rouse 2007).

Indeed, providing direct, context-specific examples of practice has been emphasized as crucial in developing EBP in TEL research (Schrum et al. 2005). In this respect, TEL research is no different from other areas of educational research, where the emphasis is on the importance of considering not only 'what works', but in what contexts something might work and for whom. However, one of the particular dangers with TEL research lies in its tendency to focus on a 'technologically determinist perspective ... which takes insufficient account of the social and cultural contexts which support the technology use' (Abbott 2007, 7). Consequently, there is often a focus on the wonder of the widget without evaluating the pedagogical context within and around the use of the technology (Crook 1991). Fisher, Higgins, and Loveless (2006) discuss the power of direct illustrations of practice through using ' ... digital video for capturing, observing and reviewing critical moments' (25). Their focus is on the affordances of digital technologies for *knowledge building* in the context of teacher learning, but their analysis is central to our argument about the potential value of digital stories as part of a co-constructed evidence base.

In particular, if teachers are to become active agents in their own research, then they need to build their knowledge about what works with *their* learners, in *their* own learning environment. As we have argued earlier, digital technologies provide a way to capture and reflect on practices, and learning, in a way that brings tacit or informal knowledge to the fore (Fisher, Higgins, and Loveless 2006). Regarding knowledge creation (rather than knowledge exchange or transfer), McFadyen and Cannella (2004) argue that ' ... knowledge creation ... is more dependent on the combination and sharing of tacit knowledge' (737). If we accept that knowledge creation is central to the building of an authentic evidence base, then methods to support the elicitation of tacit knowledge that convert 'intuitions or images ... into tangible statements ... ' (Rynes, Bartunek, and Daft 2001, 348) can be powerful tools for making knowledge (evidence) explicit and implementable, including in TEL environments.

Increasingly, the implementation of knowledge constitutes a key prerequisite of TEL, especially of environments relying on Artificial Intelligence (Porayska-Pomsta et al. 2013), as is the case in ECHOES. Therefore, methods for supporting knowledge creation can play a valuable role in helping practitioners to acquire a different understanding of their practice, to see and imagine their practice differently (De Vries 1990; Biesta 2007), and can inform the new and pedagogically more robust generations of TEL. Digital technologies can provide both the stimulus for developing and enhancing teaching and learning practices as well as the means through which those practices can be made manifest for further learning and reflection. Both features were incorporated into the Shape project.

Nevertheless, our experiences also show that not all teachers and schools may be ready for knowledge co-creation; whilst Radlett Lodge were engaged and enthusiastic from the start, and supported staff and pupil engagement with the project, they were still unsure initially about the creation of the digital stories due to space and logistical constraints, as well as concerns about fulfilling the research team's expectations about producing digital stories. Some of the other schools involved in the project preferred a more typical role in the research, that is, with members of the research team taking the lead in organizing, implementing and recording TEL sessions, and in developing the content of the digital stories. One of the key objectives of the project was to enable teacher autonomy and judgement, yet teachers themselves were often reluctant to see themselves as knowledge creators. Some were keen to look at the EBPs for research and then to look at how to transfer this evidence to their own practice. This indicates that although teachers and school staff want to grapple with how to deal with knowledge transfer, they may find knowledge co-creation much more complex and difficult. McFadyen and Cannella (2004) note that

> In knowledge creation, information exchange is frequently emergent, in that partners to the exchange are often unable to articulate, a priori, the specific knowledge that they need. (737)

We suggest that this emergent property of knowledge co-creation can offer creativity, support risk taking and can develop agency and empowerment, but it can also be felt as uncomfortable, unsure and perhaps too risky in an environment where pressure on schools and teachers to meet standards is substantial. As researchers, we need to recognize that a more democratic participatory research space may offer important epistemological opportunities, with a positive impact on the quality of evidence created (Groundwater-Smith and Mockler 2007). However, such a collaborative space may not be appropriate for all and we need to accept that there is a continuum of 'readiness' for participation along which both researchers and schools need to travel in order to negotiate different roles and expectations (Seale, Nind, and Parsons 2014).

Conclusions

Overall, the process of engagement with the school, via the development of digital stories, was powerful, informative and challenging. Teachers were enabled to share their experiences and views and they supported children's learning in creative and flexible ways; the digital stories fostered reflection and critique of the teaching and learning opportunities for pupils who were afforded through the use of the new TEL environments. As argued throughout the paper, the stories themselves can be viewed as evidential artefacts, reflecting 'indigenous' local contexts and practices of TEL use, which are central features of demonstrating e-inclusion practices (Abbott 2007), and they can be used to generate authentic evidence in the field of TEL (Schrum et al. 2005). However, the final creation of the stories was also labour intensive (for the research team), necessitating considerable investment in time and resources not initially envisaged when setting up the project. This was because we had assumed that teachers and schools would want to take more control over the generation of the stories, but their own time constraints, as well as uncertainty about their own roles in knowledge creation, meant that the story-editing and production were more the responsibility of the research team than we had planned.

In addition, by focusing on the importance and relevance of the development of research strategies that are more participatory and endorsed by both researchers and community providers, Kasari and Smith (2013) caution that the learning outcomes for children might become less of a focus than the process itself. This aligns with Schrum et al.'s (2005, 204) argument for a 'platinum standard' in school-based TEL research focusing on beliefs, practices and learning outcomes. The Shape digital stories enabled us to provide insights into the first two, and some indicators about the third. However, in order also to be able to demonstrate reliably particular learning outcomes for individual students, there is a need to triangulate the evidence from the stories with independent data about progress, preferably mapped to the pupil's IEP. This additional step would not necessarily be difficult to achieve given that schools gather such data all of the time. Crucially, in the context of developing authentic participatory research approaches with schools, this would not require formal research constraints on timing, frequency or the pedagogy of classroom-based TEL, thereby reflecting and respecting the complexity of real schools and classrooms (Rudduck and Hopkins 1985; Schrum et al. 2005).

Acknowledgements

We would like to thank staff, pupils and parents at the following schools: Ashgrove, The Hollies, Radlett Lodge, Topcliffe Primary and Trinity Fields. We would also like to thank the entire Shape team. The Shape team was led by Karen Guldberg as PI, with Sarah Parsons, Kaśka Porayska-Pomsta and Wendy Keay-Bright as C-Is, and with Lila Kossyvaki, Marilena Mademtzi, Ben Ewart-Dean as researchers and Rachel Townzen and Jamie Makower as interns. Rachael Lee co-ordinated the work of the practitioners at Radlett Lodge and created the digital stories in partnership with the teachers, children and young people there. We extend our thanks to them all.

Disclosure statement

No potential conflict of interest was reported by the authors.

Funding

The research reported in this paper was funded by the Economic and Social Research Council [grant number ES/J011207/1].

References

Abbott, C. 2007. *e-Inclusion: Learning Difficulties and Digital Technologies*. Bristol: Futurelab. Accessed August 5, 2014. www.futurelab.org.uk

Andrews, M., C. Squire, and M. Tamboukou, eds. 2013. *Doing Narrative Research*. London: Sage.

BERA-RSA. 2014. *Research and the Teaching Profession: Building the Capacity for a Self-improving Education System*. Accessed June 5, 2014. www.bera.ac.uk.

Biesta, G. 2007. "Why 'What Works' Won't Work: Evidence-Based Practice and the Democratic Deficit in Educational Research." *Educational Theory* 57 (1): 1–22.

Biesta, G., J. Allan, and R. Edwards. 2014. *Making a Difference in Theory. The Theory Question in Education and the Education Question in Theory*. Abingdon: Routledge.

Black-Hawkins, K., and B. Amrhein. 2014. "Valuing Student Teachers' Perspectives: Researching Inclusively in Inclusive Education?" *International Journal of Research and Method in Education* 37 (4): 357–375.

Black-Hawkins, K., L. Florian, and M. Rouse. 2007. *Achievement and Inclusion in Schools*. London: Routledge.

Christie, D., and I. Menter. 2009. "Research Capacity Building in Teacher Education: Scottish Collaborative Approaches." *Journal of Education for Teaching: International Research and Pedagogy* 35 (4): 337–354.

Corman, S. R. 2013. *The Difference Between Story and Narrative.* Accessed December 9, 2014. http://csc.asu.edu/2013/03/21/the-difference-between-story-and-narrative/.

Cornwall, A., and R. Jewkes. 1995. "What is Participatory Research?" *Social Science and Medicine* 41 (12): 1667–1676.

Crook, C. 1991. "Computers in the Zone of Proximal Development: Implications for Evaluation." *Computers and Education* 17 (1): 81–91.

Damschroder, L. J., D. C. Aron, and R. E. Keith. 2009. "Fostering Implementation of Health Services Research Findings into Practice: A Consolidated Framework for Advancing Implementation Science." *Implementation Science* 4 (1): 50.

Daniels, H. 2001. *Vygotsky and Pedagogy.* London: Routledge Falmer.

Denzin, N. K., and Y. S. Lincoln, eds. 2011. *The SAGE Handbook of Qualitative Research.* London: Sage.

De Vries, G. H. 1990. *De Ontwikkeling van Wetenschap* [The Development of Science]. Groningen: Wolters Noordhoff.

Dingfelder, H. E., and D. S. Mandell. 2011. "Bridging the Research-to-practice Gap in Autism Intervention: An Application of Diffusion of Innovation Theory." *Journal of Autism and Developmental Disorders* 41 (5): 597–609.

ESRC. n.d.-a. *Knowledge Transfer Partnerships.* Accessed August 5, 2014. http://www.esrc.ac.uk/collaboration/knowledge-exchange/KT-partnerships.aspx.

ESRC. n.d.-b. *Knowledge Exchange.* Accessed August 5, 2014. http://www.esrc.ac.uk/collaboration/knowledge-exchange/.

Fisher, T., C. Higgins, and A. Loveless. 2006. *Teachers Learning with Digital Technologies: A Review of Research and Projects.* Report 14: Futurelab series. Accessed June 22, 2014. http://archive.futurelab.org.uk/resources/publications-reports-articles/literature-reviews/Literature-Review129.

Goswami, U. 2006. "Neuroscience and Education: From Research to Practice?" *Nature Reviews Neuroscience* 7 (5): 406–413.

Groundwater-Smith, S., and N. Mockler. 2007. "Ethics in Practitioner Research: An Issue of Quality." *Research Papers in Education* 22 (2): 199–211.

Grove, N. November 28, 2013. "Taking Part by Telling Stories." Presentation at towards equal and active citizenship: pushing the boundaries of participatory research with people with learning disabilities, ESRC seminar series, University of Southampton.

Gubrium, A. 2009. "Digital Storytelling: An Emergent Method for Health Promotion Research and Practice." *Health Promotion Practice* 10 (2): 186–191.

Hagel, J. 2013. "Moving from Story to Narrative." Conference presentation. Accessed December 9, 2014. http://schedule.sxsw.com/2013/events/event_IAP16120.

Hall, L. 2014. "'With' not 'About' – Emerging Paradigms for Research in a Cross-cultural Space." *International Journal of Research and Method in Education* 37 (4): 376–389.

Hammersley, M. 2005. "Is the Evidence-based Practice Movement doing more Good than Harm? Reflections on Iain Chalmers' Case for Research-based Policy Making and Practice." *Evidence and Policy: A Journal of Research, Debate And Practice* 1 (1): 85–100.

Hargreaves, D. H. 2007. Teaching as a Research-based Profession: Possibilities and Prospects (The Teacher Training Agency Lecture 1996). In *Educational Research and Evidence-based Practice*, edited by M. Hammersley, 3–17. London: Open University and Sage.

Harrison, S., P. Sengers, and D. Tatar. 2011. "Making Epistemological Trouble: Third-Paradigm HCI as Successor Science." *Interacting with Computers* 23 (5): 385–392.

Hill, M. F., and M. A. Haigh. 2012. "Creating a Culture of Research in Teacher Education: Learning Research within Communities of Practice." *Studies in Higher Education* 37 (8): 971–988.

Houston, N., H. Ross, J. Robinson, and H. Malcolm. 2010. "Inside Research, Inside Ourselves: Teacher Educators Take Stock of Their Research Practice." *Educational Action Research* 18 (4): 555–569.

Kasari, C., and T. Smith. 2013. "Interventions in Schools for Children with Autism Spectrum Disorder: Methods and Recommendations." *Autism* 17 (3): 254–267.

Kemmis, S., R. McTaggart, and R. Nixon. 2014. "A New View of Research: Research Within Practice Traditions." In *The Action Research Planner*, 67–83. Singapore: Springer.

Labov, W. 1972. *Language in the Inner City: Studies in the Black English Vernacular*. Philadelphia, PA: University of Pennsylvania Press.

Lambert, J. 2010. *The Digital Storytelling Cookbook*. Berkeley, CA: Digital Diner Press/Center for Digital Storytelling. Accessed June 13, 2014. http://storycenter.org/books/.

Lambert, J. 2013. *Digital Storytelling: Capturing Lives, Creating Community*. 4th ed. Abingdon: Routledge.

Leibowitz, B., C. Ndebele, and C. Winberg. 2014. "'It's an Amazing Learning Curve to be Part of the Project': Exploring Academic Identity in Collaborative Research." *Studies in Higher Education* 39 (7): 1256–1269. doi:10.1080/03075079.2013.801424

Lemke, J. L. 1997. "Cognition, Context and Learning: A Social Semiotic Perspective." In *Situated Cognition Theory: Social, Neurological and Semiotic Perspectives*, edited by D. Kirshner, 37–55. New York: Lawrence Erlbaum.

Lowenthal, P. R. 2009. "Digital Storytelling – An Emerging Institutional Technology?" In *Story Circle: Digital Storytelling Around the World*, edited by J. Hartley and K. McWilliam, 252–259. Oxford: Wiley-Blackwell.

MacLeod, A., A. Lewis, and C. Robertson. 2014. "CHARLIE: PLEASE RESPOND!' Using a Participatory Methodology with Individuals on the Autism Spectrum." *International Journal of Research and Method in Education* 37 (4): 407–420.

McFadyen, M. A., and A. A. Cannella Jr. 2004. "Social Capital and Knowledge Creation: Diminishing Returns of the Number and Strength of Exchange Relationships." *The Academy of Management Journal* 47 (5): 735–746.

Menter, I., M. Hulme, J. Murray, A. Campbell, I. Hextall, M. Jones, P. Mahony, R. Procter, and K. Wall. 2010. "Teacher Education Research in the UK: The State of the Art." *Schweizerische Zeitschrift für Bildungswissenschaften* 32 (1): 121–142.

Mesibov, G. B., V. Shea, and E. Schopler, eds. 2004. *The TEACCH Approach to Autism Spectrum Disorders*. New York: Springer Science and Business Media.

Mishra, P., and M. J. Koehler. 2006. "Technological Pedagogical Content Knowledge: A Framework for Teacher Knowledge." *The Teachers College Record* 108 (6): 1017–1054.

Nind, M. 2014. *What is Inclusive Research*? London: Bloomsbury Academic.

Odom, S. L., E. Brantlinger, R. Gersten, R. H. Horner, B. Thompson, and K. R. Harris. 2005. "Research in Special Education: Scientific Methods and Evidence-based Practices." *Exceptional Children* 71 (2): 137–148.

Ogletree, B. T., T. Oren, and M. A. Fischer. 2007. "Examining Effective Intervention Practices for Communication Impairment in Autism Spectrum Disorder." *Exceptionality: A Special Education Journal* 15 (4): 233–247.

Ohler, J. B. 2013. *Digital Storytelling in the Classroom: New Media Pathways to Literacy, Learning, and Creativity*. 2nd ed. London: Sage.

Parsons, S., T. Charman, R. Faulkner, J. Ragan, S. Wallace, and K. Wittemeyer. 2013. "Commentary – Bridging the Research and Practice Gap in Autism: The Importance of Creating Research Partnerships with Schools." *Autism* 17 (3): 268–280.

Parsons, S., and S. Cobb. 2014. "Reflections on the Role of the 'Users': Challenges in a Multidisciplinary Context of Learner-centred Design for Children on the Autism Spectrum." *International Journal of Research and Method in Education* 37 (4): 421–441.

Parsons, S., and C. Kasari. 2013. "Editorial: Schools at the Centre of Educational Research in Autism: Possibilities, Practices and Promises." *Autism* 17 (3): 251–253.

Parsons, S., L. Millen, S. Garib-Penna, and S. Cobb. 2011. "Participatory Design in the Development of Innovative Technologies for Children and Young People on the Autism Spectrum: The COSPATIAL Project." *Journal of Assistive Technologies* 5 (1): 29–34.

Pellicano, E., A. Dinsmore, and T. Charman. 2014. "What Should Autism Research Focus Upon? Community Views and Priorities from the United Kingdom."*Autism* 18 (7): 756–770.

Porayska-Pomsta, K., M. Mavrikis, S. D'Mello, C. Conati, and R. Baker. 2013. "Knowledge Elicitation Methods for Affect Modelling in Education." *International Journal of Artificial Intelligence in Education* 22 (3): 107–140.

Robin, B. R. 2008. "Digital Storytelling: A Powerful Technology Tool for the 21st Century Classroom." *Theory Into Practice* 47 (3): 220–228.

Rudduck, J., and D. Hopkins.1985. *Research as a Basis for Teaching – Readings from the Work of Lawrence Stenhouse*. London: Heinemann Educational Books.

Rynes, S. L., J. M. Bartunek, and R. L. Daft. 2001. "Across the Great Divide: Knowledge Creation and Transfer Between Practitioners and Academics." *The Academy of Management Journal* 44 (2): 340–355.

Schrum, L., A. Thompson, D. Sprague, C. Maddux, A. McAnear, L. Bell, and G. Bull. 2005. "Advancing the Field: Considering Acceptable Evidence in Educational Technology Research." *Contemporary Issues in Technology and Teacher Education* 5 (3/4): 202–209.

Seale, J., M. Nind, and S. Parsons. 2014. "Special Issue Editorial: 'Inclusive Research in Education: Contributions to Method and Debate." *International Journal of Research and Method in Education* 37 (4): 347–356.

Shohel, M. M. C. 2012. "Nostalgia, Transition and the School: An Innovative Approach of Using Photographic Images as a Visual Method in Educational Research." *International Journal of Research and Method in Education* 35 (3): 269–292.

Taylor, C. A., Y. Downs, R. Baker, and G. Chikwa. 2011. "'I did it my way': Voice, Visuality and Identity in Doctoral Students' Reflexive Video Narratives on their Doctoral Research Journeys." *International Journal of Research and Method in Education* 34 (2): 193–210.

Thomas, G. 2013. "A review of Thinking and Research About Inclusive Education Policy, with Suggestions for a New Kind of Inclusive Thinking." *British Educational Research Journal* 39 (3): 473–490.

Thomas, G., and R. Pring, eds. 2004. *Evidence-based Practice in Education*. Berkshire: Open University Press.

Vesterinen, O., A. Toom, and S. Patrikainen. 2010. "The Stimulated Recall Method and ICTs in Research on the Reasoning of Teachers." *International Journal of Research and Method in Education* 33 (2): 183–197.

Walmsley, J. 2004. "Inclusive Learning Disability Research: The (Nondisabled) Researcher's Role." *British Journal of Learning Disabilities* 32 (2): 65–71.

Studying professional knowledge use in practice using multimedia scenarios delivered online

Patricio Herbst[a] and Daniel Chazan[b]

[a]School of Education, University of Michigan, 610 East University, Ann Arbor, MI 48109-1259, USA; [b]College of Education, University of Maryland, College Park, MD 20742, USA

We describe how multimedia scenarios delivered online can be used in instruments for the study of professional knowledge. Based on our work in the study of the knowledge and rationality involved in mathematics teaching, we describe how the study of professional knowledge writ large can benefit from the capacity to represent know-how using multimedia representations of practice and alternatives to it. These instruments can be used to study what professionals notice and decide to do in practice in ways that improve upon earlier uses of written representations of professional scenarios or videorecorded episodes. In particular, storyboards and animations of nondescript cartoon characters can be used to explore professional knowledge variables systematically while the multimodal representation of human activity in context ensures the face validity of questions.

Introduction

We describe the potential that rich media authoring and internet delivery have to transform research on professional knowledge. We are particularly interested in professional knowledge from professions whose practice involves relating to people and relying on knowledge that is often tacit; following Cohen (2005), we refer to those as *professions of human improvement*. Teaching mathematics is both a key example of a human improvement profession and the area where we ground our work; others human improvement professions include clinical medicine, legal counselling, ministry and psychological therapy. With somewhat similar meaning, Grossman et al. (2009) have written about *relational practices* including counselling, ministry and teaching. In all of those professions, some precise technical knowledge (of biology, law, scripture, subject-matter, etc.) is involved but is not sufficient; competence relies crucially on a relational know-how: Practitioners often have to come up with appropriate ways to address and relate to their clients, they have to use judgment in setting goals and matching them with means, but their actions are contingent on what their clients do. In these professions, action requires know-how whose validity rests not so much on physical laws, but on sociotechnical activity norms and professional obligations. Changes in the scale of demands for service (e.g. more human services are needed than in prior generations) and in standards for professional practice (e.g. clinicians are now expected to educate patients and involve them as agents in their recovery in addition to diagnose and treat them, teachers are expected to devolve to students responsibility for their learning and make instruction more student-centered), in professional credentialing (e.g. professional schools are increasingly expected to develop and assess professional skill rather than merely select smart people or transmit academic knowledge) and in performance standards (e.g. there are increased demands of measurement and attention to effectiveness in education, patient satisfaction in medical care, etc.) have created a practical need to identify and describe such know-how, and to improve it as part of the work of improving professional practice (Gilliam and Frede 2012; Kominski 2013).

From the perspective of human service professions that at some point need to distinguish some ways of doing things as knowledgeable and disseminate those ways of doing things as best practices to new generations of professionals, it seems important to ground such axiological and pedagogical work in descriptions of actual professional practice rather than on general values or orientations. It therefore seems essential to do research that unearths and describes the knowledge implicit in actual practice as a step towards the development of more prescriptive professional discourses. This is more preferable than the development of visions of best practice that are disconnected from actual practice because a grounding in actual practice can maintain the project of professional improvement within the realm of the possible, as piecemeal improvements that build on existing structures or that adapt existing practices (Tyack 1995). Considering this descriptive question (to identify the knowledge) as fundamental, we follow Buchmann's (1987) practice of speaking about *teaching knowledge* rather than *teacher knowledge* and generalize it to talk about *professional knowledge* rather than *professionals' knowledge*. It is likely that professionals hold at least part of that knowledge individually while other parts may be embodied in group activity structures (Cook and Brown 1999), but at this stage it is less important to gauge the extent to which individual professionals have more or less knowledge than their peers than to consider professionals as key informants on the nature of the knowledge of their profession. While professional knowledge may be explicit or tacit, individually or group held (Cook and Brown 1999), it is important to identify this knowledge, and describe what it is and how it functions in order to be able to design and test ways of improving it.

One way this professional knowledge can be described is in terms of the norms, obligations and resources for professional practice. We have elaborated on these constructs in other pieces (e.g. Herbst and Chazan 2012) in the context of our approach to the study of the practical rationality of mathematics teaching. This approach attempts to combine tacit expectations (norms) of the role professionals play in the professional situations they participate in, more explicit general demands (obligations) that characterize their professional position vis-à-vis the expectations of its stakeholders, and more personal characteristics that account for individual differences in competence and style (e.g. knowledge, skills, beliefs, etc.). Our theory accounts for professional practice as the execution of actions that for the most part satisfy the norms of situations, peppered by occasional actions that depart from such norms in ways that are justifiable by recourse to obligations. This approach permits the reconciling of considerations of individual uniqueness and free will with the social and professional pressures to conform to customary patterns of interaction.

As a contribution to the improvement of professional practices, our account of practical rationality locates two possible levers for improvement (changes in personal resources and changes in situational structures) and it describes the process of enacting improved instruction as the enactment of justifiable breaches of norms or the adaptation to new, justifiable norms (in new professional situations).

Our use of the word *norm* tries to capture the sense to which recurrent professional practices rely on expectations for action. We use the word *norm* along with other scholars (e.g. Pepitone 1976) where others have used *rules* (e.g. Much and Shweder 1978; Taylor 1993) or *routine actions* (e.g. Garfinkel 1964). While those uses may be distinguished when considered in a greater depth, for our purposes, we take them as similar and oriented to the description of socially expected patterns of action that an observer represents in a law-like proposition. Unlike the instructions of a computer programme, however, norms do not dictate action; instead, not only action follows from norms, but action also transforms norms, for example, by elaborating their circumstances of use (Taylor 1993, 56). Practice is irreducible to rules inasmuch as practitioners construct their existence coping with the stuff of life in ways that do not deliberately follow rules; but practice can be described *as if* it was governed by a set of norms that regulate performance retroactively: Validating (as meeting or not meeting expectations) a range of possibly different ways of doing things; these norms are for the most part tacit, but become apparent when breached (Garfinkel 1967; Mehan and Wood 1975). We believe that such a notion of norm manifests itself not in the recurrence of observable behavioural regularities but in the existence of repairs to behaviours that breach expectations (see Rouse 2007) can help account for the concomitance of, on the one hand, the original experiences lived by individual practitioners and, on the other hand, central tendencies of members of professional groups to act in ways that resemble each other. To investigate professional knowledge, we consider it important to account for professional situations and their norms.

Thus our account of practical rationality, pivoting on that notion of norm, asserts a position that differs from individualist and deterministic accounts of professional action: Neither original expression of self nor blind execution of rules, professional action is constructed as agents create unique, justifiable responses to norms of situated activities. We have taken the liberty to explain what we mean by norm and why they matter in the investigation of professional knowledge because such conceptualization has important methodological consequences that take us directly to the focus of this paper in the context of this special issue. The question is, How can researchers ground empirically the notions of norms and obligations? While case study work (including ethnographic observation and interviewing) has served to develop these theoretical ideas, the empirical grounding of the theory has required us to consider what sort of instrument might allow the aggregation of data that could be used for proposing and testing conjectures about the rationality of practices. We will show how multimedia online questionnaires have supported such effort for the case of understanding tacit professional knowledge of practicing mathematics teachers.

Three background techniques: observation of intact settings, survey of practitioners and breaching experiment

Three canonical techniques from social science research are in the background of our discussion. Our present conception of multimedia online questionnaires has been a way of overcoming the difficulties those techniques present in the work of accruing data to test hypotheses about norms in the practice of mathematics teaching. The first of these techniques is the observation of professional behaviour aimed at detecting behavioural regularities. The second is the survey of professionals aimed at obtaining their recognition of descriptions of norms or obligations. The third is the ethnomethodological breaching experiment.

The researchers associated with the TIMSS (Trends in International Mathematics and Science Study) Video Study (Stigler and Hiebert 1999) have shown how the observation of professional behaviour can lead to documenting regularities in teaching, which they labelled *teaching scripts*. Teaching scripts are 'a commonly accepted and predictable way of structuring a classroom session and sequencing the instructional activities' (Stigler and Hiebert 1999, 127; see also Santagata and Barbieri 2005; Santagata and Stigler 2000) and claimed that these teaching scripts differ across cultures. One possible way to document norms in teaching could be the observation of such regularities in intact lessons. The observation of intact lessons seems particularly fruitful as a source for the comparison of large grain size differences among teaching across different cultures (e.g. the presence of activity types or the order among classroom segments describable after particular activity types). But the examination of the phenomena we have called norms is more challenging. While the proposition of teaching scripts relies on the recurrence of behavioural observations, the proposition of norms relies on the recurrence of participants' expectations of actions; as Mehan (1979) showed, classroom observations can be the source of empirical material for such work, but it calls for more detailed examination, for example, the recurrent observation of a single teacher across the year. In addition to the lack of independence of the observations, the norms observed (in Mehan's case, the I–R–E, or initiation-reply-evaluation recitation pattern) are still of a grain size larger than what we would want.

A second technique of interest could be described in general as a self-report survey of teaching practices, used frequently in large-scale studies. For example, Smith, Desimone, and Ueno (2005) used selected items from the NAEP (National Assessment of Educational Progress) Teacher Questionnaire that could help understand the characteristics and frequency of teachers' practices related to teaching conceptually or procedurally. The items used to measure the extent to which teachers used conceptual teaching strategies asked teachers for the frequency of practices stated in general (e.g. 'how often students ... talk to the class about their mathematics work'). While this type of self-report instruments can achieve reliability and validity as measures of instructional practice, they describe practice as depending on general principles that the respondent must recognize explicitly. The extent to which practice responds to such general rules has been questioned (see Finch 1987). In our own attempts at using this kind of instruments to measure teachers' recognition of norms for the presentation of proof problems in the teaching of high school geometry, reliability was low when the practices were smaller in grain size but described at a similar level of abstraction (see Herbst, Kosko, and Dimmel 2013).

The third technique is what ethnomethodologists called the *breaching experiment* (Garfinkel 1967; Mehan and Wood 1975), which uses the word *experiment* in the sense of an instance in which the phenomenon is shown (as in Francis Bacon's *crucial experiment*) rather than in the sense of random assignment of participants to conditions. Ethnomethodologists' interest in understanding the tacit order beneath routine practices is fulfilled by proposing defaults or hypotheses about ways of doing things that go without saying. These hypotheses are verified through immersing participants in instances of those practices where some of their underlying defaults are flouted, and observing how participants repair (i.e. notice and elaborate) the alteration of the normal situation. In our earlier work, we had drawn inspiration from that approach to examine qualitatively the video records from teaching interventions (Herbst 2003, 2006).

The three described techniques have been in the background as we sought to develop means to study the practical rationality of mathematics teaching. We describe these means chronologically: While we have ended with online multimedia question-naires, we consider worthwhile to start from where the journey began.

Thought experiments

Heidegger notes that the skill in coping with the demands of equipment (seen broadly to include any instrument of being) becomes apparent in cases of disruption (Dreyfus 1991). Consider the voice of the practitioner as one such instrument and imagine for a moment that we could take momentary control of the voice of a practitioner, effec-tively making him or her say something that, hypothetically, breached a norm, for example, making the practitioner state an algebra word problem about vehicle encoun-ters without providing any numbers. After the practitioner states the problem in that way, they regain control of their actions. We could expect a range of repairs: a rejection of the situation (e.g. I don't know what happened to me; let me give you another problem), overt recognition to the students (e.g. this problem is different than what you are used to) or subtler suggestions (e.g. how could you represent the velocities of these cars?). In many ways, when some researchers started doing 'first person research' (Ball 2000), by becoming classroom teachers themselves and recording their practice (Ball 1993; Chazan 2000; Heaton 2000; Lampert 1985, 1990, 2001) they were engaging in a feasible and more ethically defensible version of that thought experiment. They went into the classroom with goals to create novel classroom dynamics and to understand from the inside (observing student reactions as well as their own, as recorded in journals) what it felt to teach in that way, thus documenting the kinds of teaching problems and opportunities that come to the surface when the norms of instruction are changed. Herbst (2003, 2006) use of *instructional experiments*, a design experiment that induced perturbations on the natural variability of teaching through curricular choices present in replacement lessons or units pursued similar goals.

Motivated by the goal in the education research community to move education research towards the gold standard of experimental research (Towne and Shavelson 2002), we posed to ourselves the question of how could research on the norms and dis-positions of teaching be done at scale (see Herbst and Chazan 2011, for bits of history of the Thought Experiments in Mathematics Teaching project that started in 2002). We envisioned at the time that the Internet could help create and deliver vicarious experi-ences for teachers where they could be immersed in a breaching experiment and that their response could be tracked in ways that might help understand the practical ration-ality of mathematics teaching. But we had to proceed in stages to maintain our capacity to recognize the data when we saw it.

Designing a technique to study the norms of instructional situations

Our first approach to a virtual breaching experiment was offline, but included as a main component the notion that one could virtually immerse practitioners in an instance of a professional situation, by showing them a representation of that situation. First, we used video records of lessons where the teacher[1] had flouted a norm of classroom interaction (see Herbst and Chazan 2003; Nachlieli and Herbst with González 2009). We collected conversations among participating teachers about the teaching they had observed. We analysed those conversations and enriched our understanding of how teachers might repair instruction that breached a norm (Nachlieli and Herbst with González 2009) as well as to further develop the theory, observing that practitioners might see breaches of norms as justifiable (Weiss, Herbst, and Chen 2009), which led to our proposing of the notion of obligation described earlier.

By the time we were collecting such video footage for use with focus groups of teachers, in the early 2000s, digital video and software to edit it had become more widespread. With these it became possible for people like us to treat video and audio footage not as a record of a single event but as a collection of expressions in a multimodal language whose parts might be combined in different ways to tell different stories and possibly prompt different conversations. Clearly, the notion that film recording and editing is a language was not new (Metz 1974), but reaching the technical capacity to play with that language ourselves was important in terms of exploring its capacity to instrument research (as opposed to merely tell a story). We could therefore think about possibilities such as (1) if instead of having a video segment in one location of the timeline, we put it elsewhere, or replaced it with another or (2) if an audiotrack was replaced with another, how could the viewers' responses change? It also became possible to represent instructional practice (e.g. a lesson) as a series of decisions and moves – for example, by combining footage from different cases of teaching the same lesson plan into a same timeline that represented the set of possibilities afforded by a lesson. These realizations produced several artefacts and data collection trials, but the most important outcome had to do with realizing the need to push further into thinking of the need for a graphical language to create representations of professional practice. While it was thinkable that footage from different versions of a lesson could be combined to tell a story of a conceivable new version of that lesson (and hence elicit practitioners' commentary about practice), surface features (e.g. changes in clothing from one day to the next) or contextual features (e.g. the two sources of footage being from different classes) conspired against the face validity of the achieved representation. While practitioners could see the practice through its video representation, the representation itself was done in a language that visually conspired against that sense of presence. We realized the need for a more malleable visual language that could still capitalize on the multimodality and temporal nature of video.

In parallel with our collection and analysis of teacher focus group responses to video records of lessons, we secured resources to create animations of teaching scenarios that might help expand our scope of work. We were quite aware of the problems of using video to representing generality in teaching practice (Chazan and Herbst 2011) and were looking for ways to control how much a representation of practice also constituted a representation of the social and individual context in which the practice was deployed. After some experimentation with three-dimensional characters, our hunch was that nondescript, two-dimensional, cartoon characters could help represent practice, and hence prompt practitioners to disclose the rationality of practice, without encouraging explanations that reduce human doings to the mental states of the individuals involved (see Figure 1; also Herbst et al. 2011). We also expected that the use of the same set of nondescript cartoon characters could enable combinations of footage in the service of multiple representations of practice.

We thus developed animations of classroom scenarios, where teacher and students were represented using nondescript cartoon characters and human actors performed the voice track (Herbst, Nachlieli, and Chazan 2011). Not being limited to finding or

Figure 1.   The ThExpians B character set enacting a geometry instruction scenario.
(© 2015, The Regents of the University of Michigan, all rights reserved, used with permission)

recording video, we could script lessons so as to control what norms of the practice being studied would be breached. We used these with focus groups of practitioners who were experienced in teaching the content represented in the animation. As in the case of video focus groups, conversations had an open agenda where teachers discussed what they cared to discuss about the media (Nachlieli 2011). In spite of the simplified nature of the graphics, practitioners have shown that they can talk about the practice represented as if it was a case of actual practice, for example being able to project their circumstances onto the animation (Chazan and Herbst 2012). Both videos and animations have been effective in eliciting participant commentary about norms of instructional practice. In particular, in a study of the discourse employed by teachers discussing them, animations performed just as well as video in eliciting participants' statements about norms of professional practice, as measured by participants use of the modality resources of language; but animations were better than videos in eliciting modal statements of the normativity type (e.g. *should*; Herbst and Kosko 2014). At the same time that we examined the data from focus groups, we also started developing the infrastructure to take this research approach to the internet – exploring whether and how the animations could elicit similar kinds of noticing and reflection when delivered online (Chieu, Herbst, and Weiss 2011).

The notion of a *multimedia online experience* was developed to name the genre of activity that we recruited participants for – a cross between a survey and a media enhanced interview or focus group. Research participants might be individually asked to inspect a piece of media, make comments on the timeline of the media or answer questions about the media; they might also be ushered into a chat or forum and discuss the media or the questions with other participants. An online experience thus meant to use the Internet to instrument and thus enhance the technique of using representations of practice to elicit professional knowledge. In particular, it could be used to revise and hopefully improve the virtual breaching experiment technique. It added to the notion that animations of nondescript cartoon characters could immerse viewers in a breaching experiment: It added to it the notion that this immersion could be done online, with many individuals having potentially the same experience. Our initial multimedia experiences have shown heavy engagement with the practice represented as evidenced in the proportion to which forum postings refer to events in the animations (Chieu and Herbst 2013).

The initial multimedia online experiences used animations of classroom scenarios that we had scripted and directed but whose technical realization had required the work of digital artists. As a result, the authoring of a multimedia online experience was much less flexible than the authoring of a text-based survey. But in parallel we had developed *Depict*, a storyboarding tool that enabled the composition of scenarios by dragging and dropping cartoon characters on to a canvas (see Herbst and Chieu 2011). The *Depict* tool had originally been thought as a piece of software to communicate internally about stories that needed to be animated (easing our scripting process) but we started thinking of *Depict* as a tool to author the scenarios that research participants would see and respond to: If the data were comparable to what we could get with videos and animations, storyboarding with cartoon characters brought two important affordances. On the one hand, storyboarding, unlike animating, is something researchers can do and so scenario development can be a much more interactive process. On the other hand, the storyboards being xml files, their online delivery is much less affected by computing power and connectivity than video or animations are. In what follows, we elaborate on several methodological entailments of the decision to use storyboards as the media in online experiences.

Reproducing data from virtual breaching experiments through multimedia online experiences

After piloting the notion of a multimedia online experience using animations (Chieu, Herbst, and Weiss 2011), and realizing the need to integrate *Depict* into the fold of research tools (see Herbst et al. 2011), Herbst, Chazan and Chieu designed and developed the online platform Lesson*Sketch* (www.lessonsketch.org) to author and deliver multimedia online experiences. The platform combines facilities found in media authoring and archiving software, media playing and annotating software, questionnaire editing, delivering, and reporting software, and learning content management systems. Its facilities can be used not only by researchers but also by professional developers and by professionals themselves (see Herbst, Aaron, and Chieu 2013; Herbst, Chieu, and Rougée 2014) though in this paper we are only discussing the methods and technology developed for research on teaching knowledge elicited from practicing teachers.[2] While creators of multimedia online experiences could rely on found videos or on our suite of animations as they author multimedia online experiences, *Depict* allows them to create their own scenarios very easily. Lesson*Sketch*'s *Plan* tool allows researchers and developers to author agendas for experiences by dragging functionalities (such as *Media Show* or *Question*) and dropping them onto a canvas that represents the sequence of screens the end user will see (see Herbst, Aaron, and Chieu 2013). Aided by *Plan*, researchers create agendas (i.e. questionnaires) that they then use to put together experiences[3] (i.e. administrations of a questionnaire) they share with research participants.

We have used the facilities of Lesson*Sketch* to create and deliver multimedia online experiences to hundreds of participants, so far mostly for instrument development. The data collected have shown to be usable in the sense that in addition to responses to close-ended items it does produce commentary of quality comparable with that of the participants' discourse in our animation and video based focus group. These multimedia online questionnaires are thus a new generation of virtual breaching experiments.

Some issues of instrument and research design

Instrument design

By using storyboards in multimedia online experiences, we have not had to depend on finding video records of a teacher breaching a norm of an instructional situation or on developing a high-end animation. To research teaching knowledge, one can deliberately choose specific instructional situations and, within those situations, chose specific norms to study via designing scenarios that breach that norm. The design of those scenarios still requires some unique skill (i.e. the capacity to represent practice using dialogue, inscriptions and observable behaviour), but it seems that both technically and technologically we are much closer to being able to investigate practitioners' recognition of specific norms. As we do that, we have come to realize that the design space has some texture that we need to be aware of.

It is important that scenarios do not depict the moment alone when a breach happens unless such moment is one that practitioners would unproblematically recognize as separable from the stream of experience. Rather, if a storyboard includes both moments when norms are flouted and moments when norms are complied with, researchers can include contrast questions: As Dimmel and Herbst (2014) have shown, in an instrument that explored semiotic register norms concerning what teachers expect from students, the scenarios were long enough that in addition to asking general descriptive questions, participants were asked to comment on the appropriateness of two different segments of the scenario – one where the breach was included and one where there was no breach.

An insight from ethnomethodology is that participants in a situation are mutually accountable. This insight we have used originally in our research to expect that participants will repair breaches as part of the process of talking about the scenario. But it also applies to the scenarios themselves. Namely, teacher and students help each other make sense of the situation in which they are. Authentic representation of scenarios where one norm has been breached, especially to the extent that the scenario continues beyond the breach, would then call for representing what happened after, and this would expectably include some element of accountability (e.g. if the teacher breached a norm in how she presented a problem, they themselves might repair it for the students or the students might repair it with a question or comment). Clearly, the creation of a scenario requires many more decisions than that of breaching a norm. It is quite possible that a scenario might have, in addition to the breach called for by the research interest, other breaches that just help the story be compelling. To the extent that an instrument will provide analytic leverage on the problem of whether and how a norm operates in a situation, it is thus important to include not only items that breach a norm but also items that represent a balanced array of consequences of that breach, including breaches that are repaired in the scenario and breaches that are treated as unproblematic in the scenario.

The norms that are breached may apply to strategic or tactical actions. By strategic we mean actions that are done to pursue an objective after which the whole situation has been deployed. Tactical actions instead are actions that are done to handle a circumstance that presented itself once the situation has been deployed. The distinction between strategic and tactical not only gives language to describe how participants might account for breaches of norms, but also because it helps design how to study the norms for how the teacher might respond to students' work. We have seen through our work that creating items that probe strategic norms is somewhat easier than creating items that probe tactical norms. For example in creating items that probe norms about how a teacher responds to the ways in which students solve equation tasks, several contingencies needed to be considered in making the scenarios: (1) that the teacher would respond normatively to students' normative answers, (2) that the teacher would flout the norm (i.e. repair) when responding to students' normative answers, (3) that the teacher would not repair a student's breach of the norm and (4) that the teacher would repair a student's breach of the norm. Here, the tactical norm of interest is the one breached in (3) but the other alternatives help provide contrasts so that participants' reactions to (3) could be pondered (see Chazan and Lueke 2009).

Research design

The classic breaching experiment and our first generation of virtual breaching experiments (using videos or animations with face to face groups of teachers) were experiments in Bacon's sense – a demonstration of what the phenomenon looks like. While important for the purpose of revealing the existence of norms for professional action, their limited number could hardly serve to assess the strength of norms, let alone individual differences in norm recognition. The second generation of virtual breaching experiments (online experiences including storyboarded scenarios that breached norms) could potentially have many individuals participate in the same experience and thus allow us to quantify the extent to which individual professionals recognized the norm. In this context two things have become possible: To develop instruments that purport to measure the extent to which professionals recognize a norm and to use experimental design to reveal the existence of a norm.

On the first matter, to develop instruments that measure the extent to which professionals recognize a norm, the basic observation is tied to the second point made above: When participants respond to a scenario that breaches a norm, we would like to ascertain that their responses are reactions to the breach of the norm rather than to idiosyncrasies of the scenario itself. Having multiple items that can be valid cases of breach of the same norm but different amongst themselves in regard to their storylines (e.g. the action taken to breach the norm is different, contextual details are different, specific aspects of the mathematics are different) can be useful to develop a composite norm recognition score. Herbst et al. (2013) show an example of this sort of instrument.

On the second matter, to test whether a hypothesized norm is indeed the norm, one could randomly assign participants to one of two conditions. One condition includes scenarios that represent the situation but where there is a breach of the norm being examined. The other condition includes scenarios that match most of the storyline of the former but where the norm is not breached. In both cases, responses can be examined for the presence or absence of repairs as well as for the ratings of appropriateness; participant scores per item can be aggregated, and one can test for the difference of means. Dimmel and Herbst (2014) used that design to explore semiotic norms in the doing of proofs in high school geometry. In that case, the virtual breaching experiments are indeed experiments in the sense of social science research.

Other uses of online multimedia questionnaires

The preceding discussion describes how we have developed the notion of a multimedia online questionnaire to bring to scale virtual breaching experiments. In doing so, the stimulus has been represented through storyboards where the research participants read speech balloons. And the participants' responses have been restricted completely to participants' language choices in response to open-ended questions and to their ratings in appropriateness questions. As we think about how multimedia online questionnaires can be enhanced, one way they could do this is by better reproducing the conditions of a virtual breaching experiment.

The research instrument can better situate the participant in the context of instruction by involving them in a more immersive environment. Animated videos with voice over could be better than storyboards with speech balloons if the respondent has means to register their embodied response as they traverse the scenario. Some of those means are already deployed in the Lesson*Sketch* platform, where participants can place virtual coloured pins along the timeline of a video possibly to identify a moment when they had a particular feeling or idea about what they saw. They can also make comments on the timeline. Chieu and Herbst (2013; see also Chieu, Aaron, and Herbst 2013) analysed forum participants' comments on the actions in an animation and discovered significant differences in the quality[4] of those comments when they were about a moment when there had been a breach of a norm compared to when they were about moments when there had not been a breach of a norm. But making written comments on the timeline of a video is only a minimal way of capturing the respondent's appraisal. Other ways of collecting data are possible with current computing facilities. For example, the software could ask for permission to record the participant's embodied experience by turning on the computer camera and microphone. While connectivity issues may still make the identification of the moments in the video that triggered the reaction we can expect that these issues will be resolved with time. There is however a need to develop systematic ways of reading orientational meanings and appraisals from body images and tone of voice and to relate such semiotics to the notions of breach and repair described earlier.

Also, multimedia online questionnaires include a much larger set of possible instruments beyond virtual breaching experiments and that can be deployed with capabilities such as those of the Lesson*Sketch* platform. A slight variation of the virtual breaching experiment in which respondents are shown one representation of practice and asked to comment on it, is a comparison problem inspired on the practice of optometrists who ask patients to compare how they see with two purportedly different lenses. We have used this metaphor to design an instrument (described by Herbst, Kosko, and Dimmel 2013) in which participants are asked about what they would think more appropriate as a way of presenting a problem: They are given two versions, one that complies with the norm and another that breaches the norm, and a scale to indicate the extent to which they consider one or the other more appropriate. In general, participants could be given a stem scenario represented through a media artefact such as a storyboard, then asked to consider two possible ways of continuing the scenario, both of them represented in the same graphic language as the stem, and a scale to rate the extent to which they would consider one or the other most appropriate.

A second variation is a decision problem. Again one can think of a stem scenario that presents the situation using a media artefact and stops at a moment when the practitioner needs to make a choice for what to do. The respondent could be asked to consider a number of possibilities each of which is represented with multimedia, for example using the same graphic language as the stem, and to either choose one of them that they would consider most appropriate to do or rank them in order of preference for them personally. Kosko and Herbst (2012) describe an instrument designed to gauge the extent to which practitioners choose an action consistent with a norm when a norm is at stake and how such data can be analysed using multinomial regression.

A third variation is a branching instrument, inspired by 'choose your own adventure' books (see Vicary and Fraley 2007). Participants may be presented a stem scenario through a media artefact and the scenario may stop at a moment when the story might branch depending on a decision. The participant may be invited to consider the options and make a decision. Once the decision is made, the story may continue (for example following up on the decision made and possibly showing what might be deemed consequences of the decision made). The story might stop again and the participant be asked to make another decision, and so on. For example, an earlier decision about the problems a teacher could pose to students might be followed up with information about how students responded to the problem that the teacher posed, but then the participant could be asked about how they might respond to what the student happened to do. The extent to which normative actions chosen in later questions depend on choices made in earlier questions could then be examined statistically.

All of those possible problems are variations of the original virtual breaching experiment where the participant is only expected to comment or choose actions that have been represented for them. But with the affordances of authoring and collaboration tools available, respondents can do more, both individually and collaboratively. One example of that can be described using the *Depict* tool (Herbst and Chieu 2011). Unlike other storyboarding tools, *Depict* requires very short time investment in character design and customization,[5] and thus it permits a rapid representation of a storyline that has multiple frames. Researchers can therefore create questionnaires that ask open-ended questions such as 'what would you do next?' but whose response needs to be in the form of a depiction that shows it, particularly quoting exactly what the participant would say. Clearly, in fields like mathematics teaching where a lot of professional knowledge is embodied in ways of doing the work but not precisely codified into declarative knowledge, it can be more compelling for practitioners and more reliable for researchers to have practitioners show rather than tell that knowledge.

With the inclusion of voice and image recording capabilities, Lesson*Sketch* can also be used to collect a more embodied form of survey response to capture something closer to actual performance. Participants can be given a scenario in the form of an animation or storyboard and told that the representation will stop at a moment when they will be expected to play the part of the teacher (e.g. as soon as a student finishes putting her work on the board). The software can record the time it takes the participant to offer her contribution as well as the contribution itself which can then be examined using a variety of lenses (particularly as a speech act in classroom language). This could, of course, be thought as a turn-taking simulation where over time research participants enact the role of a teacher across a lesson while researchers play (or programme) student roles. In this sense, technology can mediate (and make available online) activities like medicine's standardized patient (Barrows 1993; see Chieu and Herbst 2011, for a description of a simulation environment).

We are aware that the encounters with representations of practice that we have been describing are only simulations of real teaching practice in schools, and not yet particularly immersive simulations. Thus, the responses that we are studying are responses to the virtual experience that the representations can evoke. The steps we have taken improve upon some of the limitations of other research techniques. But, by no means do our efforts eliminate the need to consider that the representations we use (insofar as they are treatments) and the empirical material they call forth from participants (insofar as it affords opportunities for observation and study) are still subject to valuable critique with respect to construct and external validity (Shadish, Cook, and Campbell 2002, 38).

Conclusion

We have illustrated how multimedia online experiences can be used to canvass professional knowledge. We have pointed the reader to pieces where concrete examples of such instruments have been used to collect data on professional knowledge. While the examples that we know pertain to the area of mathematics teaching where we do our research, the possibilities of the genre are open for researchers interested in professional knowledge across professions of human improvement. In areas where language choices, manner, tactics and strategy, and decisions under conflicting demands are needed, there is a need to situate research in particular practices. Yet, to be able to go beyond case studies, it is important to reproduce the particular practices for large numbers of research participants. Multimedia online questionnaires offer one approximation to solve that problem and nondescript cartoon characters offer one language for representing the practices of human improvement professionals without defaulting to the very specific characteristics of social and individual context. We expect that scenarios of professional practice and experiences that require clients to comment on or respond to those scenarios can help researchers understand issues about the knowledge of professional practice – often embedded in the temporality and multimodality of practice.

Disclosure statement
No potential conflict of interest was reported by the authors.

Funding
The work reported here has been done with the support of the U.S. National Science Foundation (NSF) grants ESI-0353285 and DRL- 0918425 to the authors. All opinions are those of the authors and do not necessarily represent the views of the Foundation.

Notes
1. It is worth noting that in some of the key sessions used in this work, a researcher taught the lessons that breached existing classroom norms.
2. Lesson*Sketch* is a platform that can be used for professional learning and a description of its affordances as such a platform would need to discuss its genealogy in relation to the vast literature on computer-based learning environments generated over the last two decades (e.g. Grabinger and Dunlap 1995). The present piece, however, is about the multimedia online questionnaire as a research technique and how Lesson*Sketch* supports its deployment.

3. An experience consists of one or more agendas and a set of parameters including the dates when the experience is available, the means of access, prerequisite experiences, etc. In Lesson*Sketch*, the *Experience Manager* tool allows the configuration and delivery of experiences.
4. This quality was assessed in terms of the presence of reflective comments and the consideration of alternative teaching actions, which were in turn found using a coding scheme derived from ideas in Systemic Functional Linguistics (see also Chieu, Kosko, and Herbst 2015; Halliday and Matthiessen 2004).
5. We describe *Depict*'s character set as *lean* in the sense that the graphics available to customize characters are sufficiently few to facilitate the author's focus on designing practices rather than characters.

References

Ball, D. L. 1993. "With an Eye on the Mathematical Horizon: Dilemmas of Teaching Elementary School Mathematics." *The Elementary School Journal* 93 (4): 373–397.

Ball, D. L. 2000. "Working on the Inside: Using One's Own Practice as a Site for Studying Mathematics Teaching and Learning." In *Handbook of Research Design in Mathematics and Science Education*, edited by A. Kelly and R. Lesh, 365–402. Mahwah, NJ: Erlbaum.

Barrows, H. S. 1993. "An Overview of the Uses of Standardized Patients for Teaching and Evaluating Clinical Skills. AAMC." *Academic Medicine* 68 (6): 443–451.

Buchmann, M. 1987. "Teaching Knowledge: The Lights that Teachers Live by." *Oxford Review of Education* 13 (2): 151–164.

Chazan, D. 2000. *Beyond Formulas in Mathematics and Teaching: Dynamics of the High School Algebra Classroom*. New York: Teachers College Press.

Chazan, D., and P. Herbst. 2011. "Challenges of Particularity and Generality in Depicting and Discussing Teaching." *For the Learning of Mathematics* 31 (1): 9–13.

Chazan, D., and P. Herbst. 2012. "Animations of Classroom Interaction: Expanding the Boundaries of Video Records of Practice." *Teachers' College Record* 114 (3): 1–34.

Chazan, D., and H. M. Lueke. 2009. "Exploring Tensions between Disciplinary Knowledge and School Mathematics: Implications for Reasoning and Proof in School Mathematics." In *Teaching and Learning of Proof Across the Grades: A K-16 Perspective*, edited by. M. Blanton, D. Stylianou and E. Knuth, 21–39. New York: Routledge.

Chieu, V. M., W. Aaron, and P. Herbst. 2013, April. "Impact of Critical Events in an Animated Classroom Story on Teacher Learners' Online Comments." Paper presented at the 2013 annual meeting of the American Educational Research Association, San Francisco, CA. Deep Blue at the University of Michigan. http://hdl.handle.net/2027.42/97551.

Chieu, V. M., and P. Herbst. 2011. "Designing an Intelligent Teaching Simulator for Learning to Teach by Practicing in the Practice of Mathematics Teaching." *ZDM – The International Journal of Mathematics Education* 43 (1): 105–117.

Chieu, V. M., and P. G. Herbst. 2013, June. "Designing Reference Points in Animated Classroom Stories to Support Teacher Learners' Online Discussions." In *To See the World and a Grain of Sand: Learning Across Levels of Space, Time, and Scale*, edited by N. Rummel, M. Kapur, M. Nathan, and S. Puntambekar. Paper presented at the 10th international conference on computer supported collaborative learning, University of Wisconsin, Madison, WI, June 16–19 (Vol. 1, pp. 89–96). International Society of the Learning Sciences.

Chieu, V. M., P. Herbst, and M. Weiss. 2011. "Effect of an Animated Classroom Story Embedded in Online Discussion on Helping Mathematics Teachers Learn to Notice." *Journal of the Learning Sciences* 20 (4): 589–624.

Chieu, V. M., K. W. Kosko, and P. Herbst. 2015. "An Analysis of Evaluative Comments in Teachers' Online Discussions of Representations of Practice." *Journal of Teacher Education* 66 (1): 35–50.

Cohen, D. K. 2005. "Professions of Human Improvement: Predicaments of Teaching." In *Educational Deliberations*, edited by M. Nisan and O. Schremer, 278–294. Jerusalem: Keter Publishers.

Cook, S. D., and J. S. Brown. 1999. "Bridging Epistemologies: The Generative Dance between Organizational Knowledge and Organizational Knowing." *Organization Science* 10 (4): 381–400.

Dimmel, J., and P. Herbst. 2014. "What Details Do Geometry Teachers Expect in Students' Proofs? A Method for Experimentally Testing Possible Classroom Norms." Proceedings of the 2014 annual meeting of the international group for the Psychology of Mathematics Education. Vancouver, BC: Simon Fraser University.

Dreyfus, H. L. 1991. *Being-in-the-World: A Commentary on Heidegger's Being and Time, Division I.* Cambridge, MA: MIT Press.

Finch, J. 1987. "The Vignette Technique in Survey Research." *Sociology* 21 (1): 105–114.

Garfinkel, H. 1964. "Studies of the Routine Grounds of Everyday Activities." *Social Problems* 11 (3): 225–250.

Garfinkel, H. 1967. *Studies in Ethnomethodology.* Englewood Cliffs, NJ: Prentice-Hall.

Gilliam, W., and E. Frede. 2012. "Accountability and Program Evaluation in Early Childhood Education." In *Handbook of Early Childhood Education*, edited by R. Pianta, 73–91. New York: Guilford.

Grabinger, R. S., and J. C. Dunlap. 1995. "Rich Environments for Active Learning: A Definition." *Research in Learning Technology* 3 (2): 5–34.

Grossman, P., C. Compton, D. Igra, M. Ronfeldt, E. Shahan, and P. Williamson. 2009. "Teaching Practice: A Cross-Professional Perspective." *The Teachers College Record* 111 (9): 2055–2100.

Herbst, P. 2003. "Using Novel Tasks to Teach Mathematics: Three Tensions Affecting the Work of the Teacher." *American Educational Research Journal* 40: 197–238.

Herbst, P. 2006. "Teaching Geometry with Problems: Negotiating Instructional Situations and Mathematical Tasks." *Journal for Research in Mathematics Education* 37: 313–347.

Herbst, P., W. Aaron, and V. M. Chieu. 2013. "Lesson*Sketch*: An Environment for Teachers to Examine Mathematical Practice and Learn about its Standards." In *Common Core Mathematics Standards and Implementing Digital Technologies*, edited by D. Polly, 281–294. Hershey, PA: IGI Global.

Herbst, P., W. Aaron, J. Dimmel, and A. Erickson. 2013, April. "Expanding Students' Involvement in Proof Problems: Are Geometry Teachers Willing to Depart from the Norm?" Paper presented at the 2013 meeting of the American Educational Research Association. Deep Blue at the University of Michigan. http://hdl.handle.net/2027.42/97425.

Herbst, P., and D. Chazan. 2003. "Exploring the Practical Rationality of Mathematics Teaching through Conversations About Videotaped Episodes: The Case of Engaging Students in Proving." *For the Learning of Mathematics* 23 (1): 2–14.

Herbst, P., and D. Chazan. 2011. "Research on Practical Rationality: Studying the Justification of Actions in Mathematics Teaching." *The Mathematics Enthusiast* 8 (3): 405–462.

Herbst, P., and D. Chazan. 2012. "On the Instructional Triangle and Sources of Justification for Actions in Mathematics Teaching." *ZDM – The International Journal of Mathematics Education* 44 (5): 601–612.

Herbst, P., D. Chazan, C. Chen, V. M. Chieu, and M. Weiss. 2011. "Using Comics-Based Representations of Teaching, and Technology, to Bring Practice to Teacher Education Courses." *ZDM – The International Journal of Mathematics Education* 43 (1): 91–103.

Herbst, P., and V. M. Chieu. 2011. *Depict: A Tool to Represent Classroom Scenarios.* Technical report. Deep Blue at the University of Michigan. http://hdl.handle.net/2027.42/87949.

Herbst, P., V. Chieu, and A. Rougee. 2014. "Approximating the Practice of Mathematics Teaching: What Learning Can Web-Based, Multimedia Storyboarding Software Enable?" *Contemporary Issues in Technology and Teacher Education* 14 (4). http://www.citejournal.org/vol14/iss4/mathematics/article1.cfm.

Herbst, P., and K. Kosko. 2014. "Using Representations of Practice to Elicit Teachers' Tacit Knowledge of Practice: A Comparison of Responses to Animations and Videos." *Journal of Mathematics Teacher Education* 17 (6): 515–537.

Herbst, P., K. Kosko, and J. Dimmel. 2013. "How are Geometric Proof Problems Presented? Conceptualizing and Measuring Teachers' Recognition of the Diagrammatic Register." In Proceedings of the 35th annual meeting of the North American Chapter of the International Group for the Psychology of Mathematics Education, edited by M. Martinez and A. Castro Superfine, 179–186. Chicago, IL: University of Illinois at Chicago. Deep Blue at the University of Michigan http://hdl.handle.net/2027.42/97761.

Herbst, P., T. Nachlieli, and D. Chazan. 2011. "Studying the Practical Rationality of Mathematics Teaching: What Goes into "Installing" A Theorem in Geometry?" *Cognition and Instruction* 29 (2): 218–255.

Halliday, M. A. K., and C. Matthiessen. 2004. *An Introduction to Functional Grammar.* New York: Edward Arnold.

Heaton, R. M. 2000. *Teaching Mathematics to the New Standard: Relearning the Dance.* New York: Teachers College Press.

Kominski, G. 2013. *Changing the U.S. Health Care System: Key Issues in Health Services Policy and Management.* San Francisco: Jossey Bass.

Kosko, K., and P. Herbst. 2012. "Evaluating Teachers' Decisions in Posing a Proof Problem." Proceedings of the 34th annual meeting of the North American Chapter of the International Group for the Psychology of Mathematics Education. Kalamazoo, MI. Deep Blue at the University of Michigan. http://hdl.handle.net/2027.42/91282.

Lampert, M. 1985. "How Do Teachers Manage to Teach? Perspectives on Problems in Practice." *Harvard Educational Review* 55 (2): 178–195.

Lampert, M. 1990. "When the Problem is not the Question and the Solution is not the Answer: Mathematical Knowing and Teaching." *American Educational Research Journal* 27 (1): 29–63.

Lampert, M. 2001. *Teaching Problems and the Problems of Teaching.* New Haven, CT: Yale University Press.

Mehan, H. 1979. *Learning Lessons: Social Organization in the Classroom.* Cambridge, MA: Harvard University Press.

Mehan, H., and H. Wood. 1975. *The Reality of Ethnomethodology.* New York: Wiley.

Metz, C. 1974. *Film Language: A Semiotics of the Cinema.* Chicago, IL: University of Chicago Press.

Much, N. C., and R. A. Shweder. 1978. "Speaking of Rules: The Analysis of Culture in Breach." *New Directions for Child and Adolescent Development* 1978 (2): 19–39.

Nachlieli, T. 2011. "Co-facilitation of Study Groups around Animated Scenes: The Discourse of a Moderator and a Researcher." *ZDM* 43 (1): 53–64.

Nachlieli, T., and P. Herbst with G. González. 2009. "Seeing a Colleague Encourage a Student to Make an Assumption While Proving: What Teachers put to Play in Casting an Episode of Geometry Instruction." *Journal for Research in Mathematics Education* 40 (4): 427–459.

Pepitone, A. 1976. "Toward a Normative and Comparative Biocultural Social Psychology." *Journal of Personality and Social Psychology* 34 (4): 641–653.

Rouse, J. 2007. "Social Practices and Normativity." *Philosophy of the Social Sciences* 37 (1): 46–56.

Santagata, R., and A. Barbieri. 2005. "Mathematics Teaching in Italy: A Cross-Cultural Video Analysis." *Mathematical Thinking and Learning* 7 (4): 291–312.

Santagata, R., and J. W. Stigler. 2000. "Teaching Mathematics: Italian Lessons from a Cross-cultural Perspective." *Mathematical Thinking and Learning* 2 (3): 191–208.

Shadish, W., T. D. Cook, and D. T. Campbell. 2002. *Experimental and Quasi-Experimental Designs for Generalized Causal Inference.* Boston, MA: Wadsworth Cengage Learning.

Smith, T. M., L. M. Desimone, and K. Ueno. 2005. ""Highly Qualified" to do What? The Relationship Between NCLB Teacher Quality Mandates and the Use of Reform-Oriented Instruction in Middle School Mathematics." *Educational Evaluation and Policy Analysis* 27 (1): 75–109.

Stigler, J. W., and J. Hiebert. 1999. *The Teaching Gap: Best Ideas from the World's Teachers for Improving Education in the Classroom.* New York: Free Press.

Taylor, C. 1993. "To Follow a Rule . . . ." In *Bourdieu: Critical perspectives*, edited by C. Calhoun, E. LiPuma, and M. Postone, 45–60. Chicago, IL: University of Chicago Press.

Towne, L., and R. J. Shavelson, eds. 2002. *Scientific Research in Education.* Washington, DC: National Academies Press.

Tyack, D. 1995. *Tinkering Toward Utopia.* Cambridge, MA: Harvard University Press.

Vicary, A. M., and R. C. Fraley. 2007. "Choose Your Own Adventure: Attachment Dynamics in a Simulated Relationship." *Personality and Social Psychology Bulletin* 33 (9): 1279–1291.

Weiss, M., P. Herbst, and C. Chen. 2009. "Teachers' Perspectives on "Authentic Mathematics" and the Two-column Proof Form." *Educational Studies in Mathematics* 70 (3): 275–293.

Disqus website-based commenting as an e-research method: engaging doctoral and early-career academic learners in educational research

Daniel Kilburn and Jonathan Earley

National Centre for Research Methods, University of Southampton, Southampton, UK

This article presents an adaptation of established qualitative research methods for online focus groups by using the *Disqus* website-based commenting platform as a medium for discussion among doctoral and early-career academic learners. Facilities allowing Internet users to comment on the content of web pages are increasingly popular on news websites, social media, and elsewhere. This research deployed this technology as a means of hosting a group discussion in response to preliminary findings from a study into the teaching and learning of social research methods. This article explores the methodological and technical considerations associated with this method and presents an analysis of the data collection process. e-Research paradata generated by the website reveal how learners engaged with the discussion, while a thematic analysis of the comments themselves explores the nature of the qualitative data generated from responses. Website-based commenting appears to have potential as a means of facilitating learners' engagement in educational e-research, especially when faced with constraints of distance, time, or access. However, methodological challenges may also arise when recruiting participants and sustaining discussion using this method.

The Internet has had a transformative impact on the way that knowledge is generated, shared, and consumed. The era of so-called Web 1.0 offered the ability to access an unprecedented corpus of information, together with the benefits of electronic communication, for millions of users. Web 2.0 then denoted a shift towards mass participation in content creation, social networking, and data sharing for billions of Internet users. This evolution has had a profound influence on education and social research, helping to overcome temporal and spatial barriers, extend participation, and foster novel means of knowledge production and exchange. As a result of two decades of methodological refinements, the Internet offers increasing opportunities for qualitative e-research to engage with learners and teachers, whether within virtual learning environments (Shaw 2013), online learning communities (de Laat et al. 2007), virtual reality (Dickey 2005), or by conducting individual (e.g. James 2007) or group (e.g. Lim and Tan 2001) interviews online. Yet, as Hine (2005) reminds us, cyberspace may also constitute a 'troubled territory' within which a combination of new and long-standing methodological obstacles must be navigated.

This article examines the challenges and opportunities arising from an adaptation of online focus group methods to engage doctoral and early-career researcher (ECR) learners utilizing *website-based commenting* via an existing platform called *Disqus*. Also known as integrated online discussion forums (Birch and Weitkamp 2010), website-based commenting is an increasingly popular means for web users to post anonymous or pseudonymous comments in response to news articles, blogs, social media, and other content. The ability to comment on web-based content has been argued to constitute a novel and democratic medium for online dialogue (Weber 2014). The method developed here aimed to capitalize upon the affordances of website-based commenting as a means of asynchronous group discussion. As with other approaches for online group interviews, this method reproduced features of face-to-face focus groups (such as a common theme, a facilitator role for the researcher(s), and opportunities for participants to pose as well as respond to questions). Website-based commenting was envisaged as a way to enhance these features by integrating group discussion within web pages that provided a substantive stimulus for discussion and response (in this case, summaries of emerging themes from earlier phases of the research).

The research itself explored how social research methods are taught on short courses provided for researchers and academics at doctoral level and beyond (Kilburn, Nind, and Wiles 2014a). Within the burgeoning literature on pedagogy for doctoral training, observers have noted that learners (and supervisors) are generally left to rely on advice books that 'ossify doctoral research and the dissertation to formulaic axioms that ultimately serve to bolster a *this-is-how-you-do-it* position' (Kamler and Thomson 2008, 513). In the UK, moves have been made to address this by identifying areas of demand for research training among doctoral and ECRs (Moley, Wiles, and Sturgis 2013). In general terms, however, doctoral learners themselves remain a comparatively understudied group (Agee and Uzuner Smith 2011). Similarly, in the case of ECRs, a limited body of research has typically focused either on issues of productivity (Williamson and Cable 2003) or on career progression (Bazeley 2003). However, comparatively little research has engaged directly with the question of how social research is taught and learnt as part of the academic career (Kilburn, Nind, and Wiles 2014b). Our research sought to address this gap through a qualitative engagement with learners' experiences and perceptions of research methods teaching and learning. The online engagement with UK-based doctoral and ECRs discussed in this article constituted a final phase in a sequential, multi-method research design, with the aim of engaging these participants in dialogue and feedback in response to themes that had already emerged from our research.

In order to situate this approach within the wider context of qualitative e-research, the first section of this article offers a brief overview of existing methods for online focus groups, followed by an introduction to website-based commenting as an alternative medium for discussion. The second section of this paper offers a methodological account of the context in which this research design was formulated, and the various methodological and technical considerations involved in the development and implementation of the research instrument. The third section of this article considers the outcomes of the research, first, in terms of how learners engaged in the website-based commenting exercise and second, in terms of the potential of the responses to yield qualitative data.

Group discussions in e-research

Online discussions constitute an established qualitative e-research method, both in education and in social research more broadly. 'Website-based commenting' offers an alternative means of convening, stimulating, and moderating such discussions.

Online focus groups

Web-based focus groups are increasingly used as a method of collecting qualitative data for social research (Hooley, Marriott, and Wellens 2012). Online discussions are also used to support teaching and learning, especially within higher education (Hammond 2005). Previous research has engaged learners in online focus groups for the purposes of qualitative e-research, with the case of distance learners (Conrad 2009; Grays, Bosque, and Costello 2008), learner-practitioners (Kenny 2005), or more broadly, for research with teachers (Sinclair 2009). Internet-based group discussion has therefore been established as an effective medium 'for the creation and elaboration of online narratives' surrounding academic life (James 2007, 973). Parallels are often drawn with the key characteristics of face-to-face and online focus groups. Turney and Pocknee (2005) adapt Krueger's (1994) criteria to define online focus groups as involving participants with a shared interest or involvement in the particular topic at hand, but who are otherwise unfamiliar to each other, comprising enough people to reflect a diversity of views, but few enough to allow focused discussion, and to be convened for the purposes of gathering qualitative data from discussion.

There are a number of rationales for convening focus groups online. Perhaps foremost is the ability to overcome temporal and geographical constraints (Turney and Pocknee 2005), while offering a neutral space for discussion in which anonymity can more easily be ensured (Mann and Stewart 2000). In the case of asynchronous online focus groups, where discussion takes place over a period of days, months, or even years, participants may also be afforded more time to reflect on and formulate responses than would be the case in conventional focus groups (Lim and Tan 2001). In turn, conducting group discussions online poses certain challenges, including the absence of non-verbal cues (in the case of text-based discussions), the need for participants to possess a degree of 'digital literacy', and the risk of discussions becoming chaotic without careful moderation (Hooley, Marriott, and Wellens 2012).

The practical conduct of online focus groups raises a number of considerations. First, as with face-to-face interviews, all participants must give full and informed consent in a recordable way (Hooley, Marriott, and Wellens 2012). Second, although methods for recruiting participants to online focus groups need not differ from face-to-face formats, Internet-based contacts are often utilized for this task. For instance, email invitations or mailing lists may be used to recruit participants. Recruitment may also take advantage of existing online communities, for instance, through respondent-driven sampling whereby invitations are snowballed through social networks (Wejnert and Heckathorn 2008). Third, as with face-to-face focus groups, the researcher will likely take an active role in facilitating and moderating online discussions (often over an extended period of time). While virtual distance may exacerbate the risk of incendiary or contentious input, experience suggests that the moderator's role may in fact be 'less interventionist and less directive' than with conventional focus groups (Turney and Pocknee 2005, 910).

Website-based commenting

Commonly used formats for online group discussions include forums or message boards, which typically require users to create an account, or the exchange of email messages, for which respondents must disclose their email address. Both of these requirements may potentially deter participation. Forums or message boards also typically occupy an entire web page, over which the researcher may have little or no control over the design. Website-based comment platforms – also referred to as integrated online discussion forums (Birch and Weitkamp 2010) – have emerged as an alternative means of incorporating discussion facilities into web pages. Website-based commenting only occupies a specified area of a web page (typically below the main content), with the content of the web page itself – whether it be a news article, blog post, video, or a social media profile – acting as the stimulus for comment and discussion.

As Weber (2014, 2) points out, commenting is now 'one of the most common forms of citizen engagement online'. Commenting on news websites is perhaps the most prominent and widespread example, with articles regularly receiving thousands of comments over a few days or even hours. Commenting facilities are also increasingly common on academic websites. Research examining commenting on science blogs, for instance, found that comments often volunteered relevant information or addressed substantive points, although some input tended towards casual 'virtual water cooler' chat (Birch and Weitkamp 2010). Studies also suggest that commenting platforms can foster dialogue and discussion, rather than one-off inputs, although 'the potential for quality discourse emerge only when a substantial amount of users participate' (Weber 2014, 2). In the case of science blogs, commenting facilities were found to provide 'places to build knowledge and collaboratively work through ideas', suggesting further potential for substantive engagement (Birch and Weitkamp 2010, 900).

Commenting as an e-research method

For this research, website-based commenting was deployed as a qualitative e-research method in order to explore experiences and perceptions of research methods teaching and learning among doctoral and ECR learners.

Research design

The online group discussion formed part of a year-long study into research methods teaching and learning for those working in or towards academic careers, which sought to explore the pedagogical processes involved in, and challenges arising from, the teaching and learning of social science research methods in this context. The research design engaged with teachers and learners through a close-up component of classroom-based research and an expert panel method in which broader or strategic issues were explored.

The close-up component comprised focus group interviews in which teachers and learners took part in video-stimulated dialogue and reflection in response to key events recorded during a day's training (see Kilburn 2014; Nind, Kilburn, and Wiles, forthcoming). The expert panel component was adapted from Galliers and Huang (2012), with the aim of engaging various groups of participants who are geographically dispersed across higher education institutions. The first group was academics involved in social research methodology at a strategic level, who were individually interviewed. The second group comprised academics involved in the teaching of research methods, who took part in face-to-face focus groups. The third group, and the focus for the online discussion, comprised doctorial and ECR learners. A key characteristic of this expert panel design was the adoption of an iterative approach – not dissimilar to the 'Delphi' method (Murry and Hammons 1995) – whereby themes from the individual interviews with the first group of informants formed the basis of the topic guide for the face-to-face focus groups, the combined themes from both of which were in turn used as a stimulus for the online dialogue.

There were a number of practical rationales for using e-research to engage doctoral and ECR learners in our study. First, these individuals are geographically dispersed in higher education institutions and research organizations across the UK. The institutions themselves may also have differing cultures for research training (Deem and Brehony 2000). Second, it was felt that e-research may offer a more accessible method for engaging with groups of adult learners whose availability may be limited. Finally, it was felt that Ph.D. and ECR learners were likely to have levels of technological access and literacy that would enable them to take part in online research.

In keeping with the iterative nature of the expert panel approach, the stimulus for the online focus group comprised key themes – outlined below – that emerged from preliminary analyses of our existing interview data around four main topic areas:

(1) Challenges for learning:
   - A skills deficit among those entering research careers
   - The inherent complexity of advanced research methods
   - Changes to the nature of postgraduate and postdoctoral research careers
(2) Provision of teaching and training:
   - The generalist short course model of methods training
   - Embedding learning within specific disciplinary or substantive contexts
   - The apprenticeship model of individual supervision
(3) Teaching approaches:
   - Deciding upon the content of methods teaching and training
   - Authenticity and applicability of the teaching materials
   - Opportunities for sharing experiences
(4) Qualities of methods teachers and learners:
   - The roles of methods teachers
   - The roles of methods learners
   - Co-learning between teachers and learners as researchers

A design for an online group discussion developed around summaries of the themes from each topic as a stimulus for discussion.

Ethical considerations contributed a final set of requirements for the research design. Approval was granted from the University's Ethics Committee on the basis that this component of the research achieved respondents' full and informed consent, afforded them the opportunity to opt out during data collection, and allowed them to maintain anonymity. As it was felt that an open-access discussion would maximize responses, ethics approval also took into account the fact that confidentiality would not be assured and the comments could be viewed by others during the period of data collection.

Developing an online discussion platform

The research design called for the discussion to be stimulated by the emerging themes from our research and it was necessary to design a bespoke set of web pages to achieve this. These would be hosted on our own institutional website (www.ncrm.ac.

uk), which is already a well-frequented resource for doctoral and ECR learners. As with many higher education websites, it also features a clear interface for navigation; is compatible with phones, tablets, and other devices; and runs on a secure platform, making it a well-suited host. Above all, however, integrating a discussion feature into own website allowed us freedom to design web pages around the summaries of themes from our research.

Previous experience with setting up and managing web based discussion was formative in the design of this research instrument. The technicalities of integrating a discussion forum into institutional websites had proved challenging in the past, as had the difficulty of engaging participants. In technical terms, forums generally do not fit within the templates of websites meaning that full control over the look and feel of the web page(s) must be sacrificed. Forums can also be more vulnerable to security threats and spam (the posting of junk messages). *Disqus*, the system that was chosen as the tool for hosting the online discussion, is a facility for uploading or posting text-based comments that can be integrated into an existing web page design. Comments are typed and edited using features built into the *Disqus* system and can be posted using a pseudonym. Once uploaded, comments appear in series. Users can either post new comments or choose to reply to existing posts (these replies are nested, meaning that they appear directly below the original comment). Commenting platforms such as *Disqus* therefore effectively turn part of a web page into a fully functional discussion forum, while retaining control over the design and content of the remainder of the page.

The task of developing the web pages that are suited to the needs of a discussion such as this was not trivial. The first stage involved the creation of the web pages themselves. A front page was required, via which all visitors would pass prior to accessing the discussion pages and on which the ethics information was provided, together with an option to give consent and proceed. Consenting respondents were then directed to a contents page allowing them to navigate among the four discussion topics (Figure 1). The discussion pages themselves each featured a brief (300-word) summary of the key themes that emerged around the given topic. These summaries also included links to other online resources relating to methods teaching and learning that were potentially of interest to respondents (such as academic blog posts, videoed lectures/presentations, or open-access papers). It was felt that providing these additional resources may help further foster participants' interest and engagement. The *Disqus* component of each discussion page then appeared directly below these summaries.

In technical terms, *Disqus* can be integrated into web pages through a series of steps. These are likely to require some web-development skills, as *Disqus* works using code in the *JavaScript* programming language. In order for the discussion to appear across multiple web pages, a web scripting language can be used to automatically insert variables into the *JavaScript*. Each page using *Disqus* requires four unique variables:

(1) A category identification code that is generated on the *Disqus* website;
(2) A text identifier for the id (also generated by *Disqus*);
(3) The web link for the page where each *Disqus* thread is; and,
(4) An appropriate web-page title.

These variables need to be embedded in a single page containing the javascript. Once the javascript has been included beneath these variables, this is where the *Disqus* features will appear on the web page.

Photos from the ESRC Research Methods Festival 2010, Copyright NCRM

Figure 1. Tiled design for a main contents page, linking to the four discussion topics.

Deployment

Following a pilot exercise in which colleagues were invited to experiment with and comment on the functionality of the *Disqus* system, the discussion web pages went live for a period of six weeks. An *ad hoc* sampling strategy was adopted for the recruitment of participants from an unknown population of doctoral and ECR learners (insofar as a comprehensive sampling frame could not be assembled). On the other hand, this population was comparatively accessible via institutional or social networks. It was therefore decided that email invitations would be circulated to potential participants by way of institutional gatekeepers (such as departmental/programme administrators), mailing lists (including NCRM's email bulletin to around 4800 addressees), information on NCRM's website (which receives around 3000 visits per month), and posts on Twitter feeds (such as #PhDChat and #ECRChat, as well as NCRM's Twitter page, with over 3500 followers). These invitations included a brief description of the research and of what participation would involve, a link to the consent 'portal' of the website, and a request to pass the invitation on to others who might be interested. As such, the sampling approach therefore combined elements of convenience sampling with the sorts of respondent-driven sampling that seeks to facilitate snowballing within participants' own social networks (Wejnert and Heckathorn 2008).

Recruitment was staggered over the six-week data collection period, with invitations circulated first via email contacts and institutional networks, before being disseminated across public communications channels. We were encouraged by learners' willingness to disseminate details of the research via their own networks, including by authoring blog posts on institutional websites (in two instances) and by sharing information via mailing lists (in two further instances). We also received 10 retweets on Twitter accounts relating to Ph.D. and ECR issues (one with over 8000 followers). This affirmed the potential to use social and institutional networks for disseminating information on e-research, although the process of generating responses was without its pitfalls as the following section illustrates.

Engagement and data collection

The discussion pages generated 26 responses from 18 respondents over a six-week period. However, these headline figures only tell part of a more complex story of how learners engaged with the discussion. The first part of this section looks beyond the responses themselves, to analyse characteristics of users' engagement with the web pages. The second part of the analysis engages with the responses to the discussion themes as a source of qualitative data and offers a closer reading of types of comments contributed by respondents.

Engaging learners

The inclusion of learners as genuine participants in – rather than subjects of – educational research addresses pressing methodological and moral issues (see the recent special issue of this journal; Seale, Nind, and Parsons 2014). A small step towards greater participation includes providing opportunities for stakeholders in the topic at hand to engage in feedback and dialogue in response to the outcomes of educational research. Our research design took this as its cue in using summaries of emerging themes from the earlier phases of the research as a stimulus for an online discussion. While the primary intention was to collect data, a secondary aim was that participants – including those who viewed the website and discussion content, but may not have responded – also had an opportunity to engage with these emerging themes at a formative stage in the research process.

Learners' engagement with the online discussion can be explored through paradata – or data pertaining to the operationalization of the research instrument itself – in the form of statistics on how visitors interacted with each of the web pages. The gathering of so-called traffic statistics is a commonplace feature of websites (such as that used by our institution) and, in this context of e-research, this provides a valuable source of paradata. These data include measures of the number of views (or *hits*) received by the web page over time, the average length of time spent on each page, and the point at which most people exited the website (provided as the *exit rate* for each page). Table 1 shows how the number of unique views (i.e. individual visitors) received by the discussion pages was substantially higher than the 26 responses may suggest. Nearly 600 views were received by the consent/information page to which all prospective respondents were initially directed, and which equated to over 200 visitors consenting to proceed to the contents of the discussion itself. On the one hand, this somewhat reinforces the stark picture of the modest number of responses (with 26 responses from 575 prospective visitors, this response rate could be as low as 3%). However, this does not fully capture how these learners – whether respondents or non-respondents – engaged with the website.

As Table 1 shows, the four discussion topics themselves received between 91 and 138 visits. Figure 2 provides a visual representation of the breakdown of the total unique page views received by each page, emphasizing the sizeable difference in views to the consent page and those by the discussion pages. It also appears that the first discussion topic received a slightly higher number of views, with less variation between the remaining three topics. Moreover, the relatively low exit rate for each of the discussion pages suggested that visitors may have also viewed more than one page before finally leaving the site (the exit rate being the proportion of visitors who leave the website entirely after viewing a given web page).

The average length of time spent on each web page is illustrated in Figure 3 and provides a more encouraging measure of visitors' engagement with the discussion pages. The longest time was spent on the first topic (3 minutes 47 seconds), which also generated the most comments (as discussed in the following section), with less time spent on the remaining three topics. It is impossible to say whether the variation in the length of time spent on the discussion pages reflects different levels of topic interest, the cumulative effect of the number of replies for certain topics, or simply the ordering of the four topics themselves. However, the average duration spent on each page suggests that people were at least remaining long enough to read the summaries of the emerging themes from our research, browse the comments, and in some cases, formulate and contribute responses.

These paradata also provide us with an insight into the distribution of visits to the discussion pages over the six-week period of data collection (Figure 4). Both visits and contributions increased substantially from the first into the second week and then peaked in week three before tailing off, reflecting others' observation that online focus groups elicited the most engagement at the beginning of the discussion (Lim and Tan 2001). This distribution of traffic to the discussion pages appears to correspond to the staggered dissemination of invitations to prospective participants. Interestingly, although visits to the web pages increased with the circulation of email invitations and information via institutional communication channels, the proportion of those visitors actually proceeding beyond the consent page remained relatively constant.

On the one hand, the insights from these paradata appear to affirm the significant challenges involved in engaging learners or other groups in e-research. The small number of responses attests to the difficulties of recruiting respondents through an open invitation, despite the potential level of topic interest, the reach of the online

Table 1. Summary paradata measures provided by website traffic statistics.

		Unique pageviews (count)	Exit rate (% of views)[a]	Time spent on page (avg.)
Consent page		575	56%	1 minute 44 seconds
Contents page		212	24%	40 seconds
Discussion pages	1	138	28%	3 minutes 47 seconds
	2	96	13%	1 minute 23 seconds
	3	91	17%	1 minute 49 seconds
	4	94	27%	2 minutes 02 seconds

[a]As estimated by Google analytics.

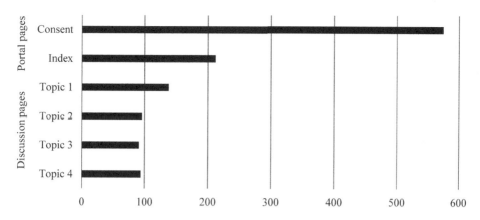

Figure 2.   Unique views to the web pages.

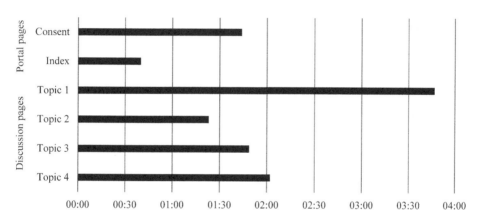

Figure 3.   Average time spent per-visit on each of the web pages.

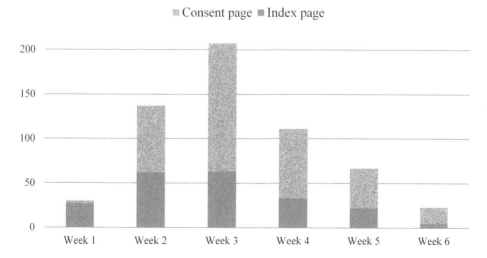

Figure 4.   Frequency of visits to the website over the six-week data collection period.

networks used to disseminate information about the research, and the relative ease of using the *Disqus* system. Perhaps most striking is the fact that these responses reflected the product of over 500 visits to the website in total. However, when considering that a secondary aim of this exercise was to engage learners with emerging themes from the research, the patterns revealed by the paradata are somewhat more encouraging. With over 150 visitors proceeding to one or more of the discussion pages, and spending an average of over two minutes viewing the pages, this suggests that the findings of our research reached a number of learners at a stage in the study when this would not otherwise have occurred.

Qualitative data

The discussion generated a 4500-word corpus of qualitative data, providing insights into the provision of methods training and reflections on the teaching and learning processes involved. The average length of the individual responses themselves was around 170 words – slightly more than 128 word average from Lim and Tan's (2001) online focus groups with teachers – with some comments extending to over 500 words. Comments reflected a wide range of perspectives from learners, although three broad types of responses were discernible. First, a number of responses either affirmed or challenged the themes from our research, typically in quite brief terms. Second, and in turn other responses elaborated upon aspects of teaching and learning in more detail, sometimes identifying areas we had perhaps overlooked, with some even volunteering hyperlinks or references to further sources of information. Third, some respondents shared personal reflections on their own experiences as learners, practitioners, or teachers of research.

Many responses took the form of comments offered in reply to particular aspects of the emerging themes that were presented as a stimulus for discussion. These contributions were typically one-off posts, rather than engagements in dialogue with other participants, and often constituted relatively brief expressions of learners' opinions. Some responses sought to affirm particular points which resonated with learners' own experiences; for instance, this comment in response to the difficulty of pitching training at the appropriate level:

> I agree with the challenges associated with planning advanced methods training. I found three quarters of the research training modules I attended as a learner far too basic for me ...

Other responses challenged aspects of our findings, such as this comment questioning the primacy of expertise as a desirable quality for teaching methods at doctoral level:

> While expertise in research methods should be a given for someone teaching research methods, contrary to the finding above, I feel that teaching ability and style is of tremendous importance ...

These replies perhaps had the most in common with comments typically left in response to content such as news articles, in that they typically offered a limited amount of elaboration in agreement or disagreement with the points raised (Weber 2014). As a result, these did not reflect the depth of responses reportedly generated by other online focus group formats (Stewart and Williams 2005). As educational researchers, these inputs from learners nevertheless proved formatting in helping to affirm, qualify, or challenge these initial findings.

A second typical of responses took the form of (often critical) elaborations the emerging themes from our research. For instance, this comment invited us to consider time pressures on doctoral students as a challenge for teaching and learning of research that did not feature in the summary of our existing research findings:

> Part of the problem is also that the PhD process is increasingly compressed. The pressure to complete within three to four years means that there's often very little time for taught courses on methods …

These responses also appeared more likely to generate further discussion, as was the case with the above point. For instance, another participant subsequently replied; 'I note "Pete's" comments about compressed timescales and suppose this is the nub of the problem'. Others raised more critical questions regarding areas they felt were not addressed in the summaries of research themes we presented. For instance, this comment challenged other discussants in terms of aspects of research methods that were *not* being spoken about:

> For me these questions rest on other issues that need to be discussed too. So, how much are we talking about particular methods/techniques and how much about methodology more broadly?

Finally, in a more practical vein, other comments of this type even volunteered additional sources of information. For instance, this participant included a reference to Reid and Petocz (2002) when discussing teachers' conceptions of statistics, in order to substantiate their argument that:

> The idea that [statistics] are simply tools is allowed to persist far too far into research methods courses and it is this epistemic simplification which limits their application.

This type of response appears to reflect others' observation that online group discussions may allow participants more time to formulate contributions that are less spontaneous and more considered (Hooley, Marriott, and Wellens 2012). As such, the detail, specificity, and criticality of some comments served as welcome reminders to us that the themes we had presented did necessarily reflect the full range of issues or concerns felt by learners.

A third type of response involved the sharing of participants' own experiences of research methods teaching and learning. Despite the fact that we were not explicitly seeking to elicit details of individual's learning contexts, many participants nevertheless positioned themselves as such, for instance; 'I am a part-time PhD student and a lecturer at a post-1992 University … ', or 'when I started my PhD I had been out of academia for ten years … '. Other participants chose to share personal experiences, for instance;

> One of the things I struggled with the most was methodology. When I started my fieldwork it was a 'learn as you go' experience. Maybe that's the nature of it. But it would have been really helpful if there was more training in the first year.

However, some responses even offered points of self-reflection:

However what I have been unhappy with myself about is that in the beginning of my PhD I felt compelled to gather quantitative data to do data analysis. I had an underlying compulsion that ONLY quantitative data analysis provides valid and objective research for a PhD ...

Compared with the majority of the responses received, the reflexive nature of these comments felt more akin to the discussions that developed from our face-to-face focus groups with learners (Kilburn, Nind, and Wiles 2014a). However, others have argued that the anonymity and physical distanciation of online environments may encourage participants to reveal personal information (Stewart and Williams 2005; Turney and Pocknee 2005). Although our research design did not expressly call for personal reflections, these added useful context, nevertheless. Moreover, this also suggests that website-based commenting may prove effective for online interviews concerning more personal or sensitive topics.

In substantive terms, the *Disqus*-based online discussion yielded valuable data in response to the emerging themes. Importantly, learners' responses did not merely reaffirm, elaborate upon, or amplify the existing findings. Rather, they encouraged us to look elsewhere, consider additional challenges associated with the academic early career, appreciate opportunities and affordances of methods learning in certain contexts, or to draw upon a broader range of examples or sources. In methodological terms, these qualitative data also yielded interesting insights into website-based commenting as an e-research method. Most notably, while the exercise was designed to elicit discussion and dialogue, the majority of the 26 contributions were one-off comments (with eight offering replies to others). This reflected acknowledged limitations of retaining or sustaining participation within online discussions (Lim and Tan 2001). On the one hand, this contrasted with face-to-face focus groups, in which both researchers and other participants can probe for elaboration or facilitate further discussion on certain points. On the other hand, the sequential nature of the *Disqus* discussion, complemented by the fact that the researchers replied to each comment, gave the data a discursive character that belied the one-off nature of many contributions. The data generated from this exercise were thus felt to have a degree of commonality with those generated from our face-to-face focus group interviews. This was the case both in terms of the structure of the data (with a balance between participants' and researchers' voices, for instance), as well as in terms of its tone (responses written in a first-person, conversational style, for instance). This meant that the data gathered using *Disqus* were amenable to the same analytical and interpretive approaches as those used for spoken data. In our case, this meant that these responses were analysed and coded alongside our face-to-face interview data using *NVivo*, with the aim that these data would be presented together within substantive research outputs.

Conclusion

The Internet has afforded new opportunities in the realms of both education and social research. Learners increasingly participate in virtual learning environments, feedback instruments, and online communities or networks, while participants in social research are increasingly engaged via online survey, focus groups, or interview methods. These instruments typically utilize existing Internet technologies, such as email or discussion forums. Technological developments in online communication, such the *Disqus* platform for website-based commenting, may therefore offer new methodological opportunities for e-research. This paper has explored one such adaptation of online focus group methods, involving the integration of *Disqus* into a series of discussion web pages in order to engage learners in themes emerging from earlier phases of our research.

This approach raised a number of practical and methodological considerations. The design of the discussion web pages required a substantial investment of time and web-development expertise. However, the *Disqus* platform allowed us to retain control over the content and appearance of the web pages, while incorporating features that enabled participants to contribute anonymously and with relative ease that were particularly valuable for an open-access online discussion. Yet, despite the accessible nature of the research instrument and the wide-ranging institutional networks used to disseminate invitations to participate, the number of responses remained lower than expected. Ease of participation and levels of recruitment did not, therefore, come hand in hand. That said, visitors' engagement with the discussion itself yielded more encouraging insights. The website paradata showed that a reasonable proportion (at least one-in-four) of those who clicked on the invitation link proceeded to view the discussion topics themselves. Moreover, these data also indicated that visitors spent several minutes reading – and in some cases, responding to – the themes presented from our research. This suggests potential for website-based commenting to engage learners in consultation, feedback, and dialogue in response to the findings of educational research, providing opportunities for formative input at a point in the research process where this would not otherwise be possible. The use of website-based commenting may thus extend the boundaries of e-research methods beyond data collection, with scope for deploying an instrument such as *Disqus* to help facilitate the sorts of public engagement sought by research funders and other bodies (see www.publicengagement.ac.uk).

The question remains, however, as to the prospects for website-based commenting as a means of collecting qualitative data. The fact that many of the responses were offered as one-off contributions, sometimes of a comparatively cursory nature, contrasts somewhat with the nature of face-to-face focus groups. On the other hand, the online format facilitated an engagement with a greater number of respondents than could be accommodated in a conventional focus group. Moreover, a number of contributions offered a greater level of depth, detail, or consideration than might be expected from a face-to-face discussion. The use of themes from our existing research findings as stimuli for responses also elicited comments that were closely tailored to the research questions, with little need for moderation. As a result, the data generated from these responses worked to amplify, complexify, or challenge our interpretations of teaching and learning. Open-access and asynchronous online discussions thus bring considerable potential to overcome constraints of time, distance, or access when engaging underresearched populations such as postgraduate or postdoctoral learners of research method. Given the considerable challenges of entering and establishing a career in social research, opportunities for dialogue between learners and education researchers in this context are rare and, as such, the affordances offered by qualitative e-research should be capitalized upon and nurtured.

Acknowledgements

This study was led by Melanie Nind (Principal Investigator) and Rose Wiles (Co-Investigator) and was supported by the Economic and Social Research Council grant for the National Centre for Research Methods Hub [grant number RES-576-47- 5001-01].

Disclosure statement

No potential conflict of interest was reported by the authors.

References

Agee, J., and S. Uzuner Smith. 2011. "Online Discussions in a Doctoral Research Methods Course: 'Like a Text by Many Authors'." *Studies in Continuing Education* 33 (3): 301–319. doi:10.1080/0158037X.2010.515574

Bazeley, P. 2003. "Defining 'Early Career' in Research." *Higher Education* 45 (3): 257–279. doi:10.1023/A:1022698529612

Birch, H., and E. Weitkamp. 2010. "Podologues: Conversations Created by Science Podcasts." *New Media & Society* 12 (6): 889–909. doi:10.1177/1461444809356333

Conrad, D. 2009. "Cognitive, Instructional, and Social Presence as Factors in Learners' Negotiation of Planned Absences from Online Study." *The International Review of Research in Open and Distance Learning* 10 (3): 1–18.

Deem, R., and K. J. Brehony. 2000. "Doctoral Students' Access to Research Cultures-are Some More Unequal than Others?" *Studies in Higher Education* 25 (2): 149–165. doi:10.1080/713696138

Dickey, M. D. 2005. "Three-dimensional Virtual Worlds and Distance Learning: Two Case Studies of Active Worlds as a Medium for Distance Education." *British Journal of Educational Technology* 36 (3): 439–451. doi:10.1111/j.1467-8535.2005.00477.x

Galliers, R. D., and J. C. Huang. 2012. "The Teaching of Qualitative Research Methods in Information Systems: An Explorative Study Utilizing Learning Theory." *European Journal of Information Systems* 21 (2): 119–134. doi:10.1057/ejis.2011.44

Grays, L. J., D. D. Bosque, and K. Costello. 2008. "Building a Better M.I.C.E. Trap: Using Virtual Focus Groups to Assess Subject Guides for Distance Education Students." *Journal of Library Administration* 48 (3–4): 431–453. doi:10.1080/01930820802289482

Hammond, M. 2005. "A Review of Recent Papers on Online Discussion in Teaching and Learning in Higher Education." *Journal of Asynchronous Learning Networks* 9 (3): 9–23.

Hine, C. 2005. "Internet Research and the Sociology of Cyber-Social-Scientific Knowledge." *The Information Society* 21 (4): 239–248. doi:10.1080/01972240591007553

Hooley, T., J. Marriott, and J. Wellens. 2012. *What is Online Research? Using the Internet for Social Science Research*, edited by G. Crow. London: Bloomsbury.

James, N. 2007. "The Use of Email Interviewing as a Qualitative Method of Inquiry in Educational Research." *British Educational Research Journal* 33 (6): 963–976. doi:10.1080/01411920701657074

Kamler, B., and P. Thomson. 2008. "The Failure of Dissertation Advice Books: Toward Alternative Pedagogies for Doctoral Writing." *Educational Researcher* 37 (8): 507–514. doi:10.3102/0013189X08327390

Kenny, A. J. 2005. "Interaction in Cyberspace: An Online Focus Group." *Journal of Advanced Nursing* 49 (4): 414–422. doi:10.1111/j.1365-2648.2004.03305.x

Kilburn, D. 2014. *Methods for Recording Video in the Classroom: Producing Single and Multi-Camera Videos for Research into Teaching and Learning*. National Centre for Research Methods Working Paper 10/14.

Kilburn, D., M. Nind, and R. Wiles. 2014a. *Short Courses in Advanced Research Methods: Challenges and Opportunities for Teaching and Learning*. National Centre for Research Methods Report.

Kilburn, D., M. Nind, and R. Wiles. 2014b. "Learning as Researchers and Teachers: The Development of a Pedagogical Culture for Social Science Research Methods?" *British Journal of Educational Studies* 62 (2): 191–207. doi:10.1080/00071005.2014.918576

Krueger, R. A. 1994. *Focus Groups: A Practical Guide for Applied Research*. Thousand Oaks, CA: Sage.

de Laat, M., V. Lally, L. Lipponen, and R.-J. Simons. 2007. "Online Teaching in Networked Learning Communities: A Multi-Method Approach to Studying the Role of the Teacher." *Instructional Science* 35 (3): 257–286. doi:10.1007/s11251-006-9007-0

Lim, C. P., and S. C. Tan. 2001. "Online Discussion Boards for Focus Group Interviews: An Exploratory Study." *Journal of Educational Enquiry* 2 (1): 50–60.

Mann, C., and F. Stewart. 2000. *Internet Communication and Qualitative Research: A Handbook for Researching Online*. London: Sage.

Moley, S., R. Wiles, and P. Sturgis. 2013. *Advanced Research Methods Training in the UK: Current Provision and Future Strategies*. National Centre for Research Methods Report. http://eprints.ncrm.ac.uk/2970/1/NCRM_Advanced_Research_Methods_Training_in_the_UK_Current_Provision_and_Future_Strategies.pdf

Murry, J. W., and J. O. Hammons. 1995. "Delphi – A Versatile Methodology for Conducting Qualitative Research." *Review of Higher Education* 18 (4): 423–436.

Nind, M., D. Kilburn, and R. Wiles. Forthcoming. "Using Video and Dialogue to Generate Pedagogic Knowledge: Teachers, Learners and Researchers Reflecting Together on the Pedagogy of Social Research Methods." *International Journal of Social Research Methodology*.

Reid, A., and P. Petocz. 2002. "Students' Conceptions of Statistics: A Phenomenographic Study." *Journal of Statistics Education* 10 (2): 1–18.

Seale, J., M. Nind, and S. Parsons. 2014. "Inclusive Research in Education: Contributions to Method and Debate." *International Journal of Research & Method in Education* 37 (4): 347–356. doi:10.1080/1743727X.2014.935272

Shaw, A. 2013. "Examining the Potential Impact of Full Tuition Fees on Mature Part-Time Students in English Higher Education." *Journal of Further and Higher Education* 38 (6): 838–850. doi:10.1080/0309877X.2013.778962

Sinclair, A. 2009. "Provocative Pedagogies in e-Learning: Making the Invisible Visible." *International Journal of Teaching and Learning in Higher Education* 21 (2): 197–212.

Stewart, K., and M. Williams. 2005. "Researching Online Populations: The Use of Online Focus Groups for Social Research." *Qualitative Research* 5 (4): 395–416. doi:10.1177/1468794105056916

Turney, L., and C. Pocknee. 2005. "Virtual Focus Groups: New Frontiers in Research." *International Journal of Qualitative Methods* 4 (2): 32–43.

Weber, P. 2014. "Discussions in the Comments Section: Factors Influencing Participation and Interactivity in Online Newspapers' Reader Comments." *New Media & Society* 16 (6): 941–957.

Wejnert, C., and D. D. Heckathorn. 2008. "Web-Based Network Sampling: Efficiency and Efficacy of Respondent-Driven Sampling for Online Research." *Sociological Methods & Research* 37 (1): 105–134.

Williamson, I. O., and D. M. Cable. 2003. "Predicting Early Career Research Productivity: The Case of Management Faculty." *Journal of Organizational Behavior* 24 (1): 25–44. doi:10.1002/job.178

Hermeneutics as a methodological resource for understanding empathy in on-line learning environments

Margaret Walshaw[a] and Wayne Duncan[b]

[a]Institute of Education, Massey University, Palmerston North, New Zealand; [b]Northern Southland College, Queenstown, New Zealand

Hermeneutics is both a philosophical tradition and a methodological resource. In this qualitative study, hermeneutics provided, simultaneously, a framework and a methodology for understanding empathy in synchronous multimedia conferencing. As a framework for the design of the study, hermeneutics supported the overriding objective to understand the human phenomenon of empathy and students' and teachers' experiences of this phenomenon. As a methodological resource, hermeneutics pointed to an approach to data collection and analysis that would allow us to honour and remain faithful to participants' stories of their experiences of empathy in on-line educational environments. In this article, we provide an explanation of the iterative approach used to interpret empathy within classroom environments devoid of face-to-face interactions. Those approaches offered increasingly deeper understandings of the ways in which people are able to perceive how others *feel* in on-line environments.

Introduction

In *Mind in Life,* Thompson (2007) speaks of empathy as a 'precondition for our experiences of inhabiting a common and inter-subjective spatial world' (391). Providing 'a viewpoint in which one's centre of orientation is one among others' (391), empathy is a necessary capability for the management of the interpersonal relationships and complex social dynamics necessary for social cohesion (Pivec 2007; Schulkin 2004). Within social communities established for formal teaching and learning purposes, empathy allows teachers and learners to build and maintain effective teaching and learning relationships (Rogers and Freiberg 1994) and to experience what some authors (Jolliffe and Farrington 2004; Mehrabian 2009) have described as a feeling of *standing in another's shoes* and *thinking like another.* How might we understand empathy in educational environments that are offered *without* face-to-face interaction? In this paper, we illustrate how the principles of hermeneutics might be used to investigate and understand the role of empathy in a synchronous educational multimedia environment.

Formalized education now transcends the barriers of distance and time as learners take advantage of educational opportunities regionally, nationally, or even globally, at any time of the day or night. By leveraging the power of information and communication technologies (ICTs), a group of collaboration tools in on-line learning environments known as synchronous multimedia conferencing (SMC) tools have come into prominence and created more flexible, interactive and content-rich conferencing options (Moore and Anderson 2003; Vonderwell and Franklin 2002). These internet-based computer technologies provide a range of real time voice, video, text and application sharing capabilities within point to point, or multipoint distributed learner environments. Importantly, SMC acknowledges the role of empathy in social interaction and learning (Finkelstein 2006).

Empathy has an important role in the teaching/learning relation, not only within face-to-face interaction but also within on-line interaction (see Holmberg 2003; Ickes 1997; Kehrwald 2008; Preece 2005). Empathic communication proceeds on the basis of backward and forward dialogic engagement. If successfully achieved, social interaction and learning can occur. These empathic engagements generate tacit, heuristic, context-bound knowledge and understandings and are able to be explored through an interpretive approach (Ajjawi and Higgs 2007).

A number of approaches, namely, those based on the frameworks of transactional distance, social presence, and cognitive distance, have been put forward by others for exploring empathetic engagements. The significant differences among these approaches arise from the way in which 'empathy' is conceptualized, variously as a *concept* within social presence (Hughes, Ventura, and Dando 2007), an *element* of absorptive capacity (Cohen and Levinthal 1990), a *social–relational mechanism* which affects the social dynamics of technology-mediated environments (Kehrwald 2008), a *construct* within cognitive distance (Nooteboom 2008), a *significant factor* in on-line social interaction (Holmberg 2003), and as a *phenomenon* within on-line textual communities (Preece 2005). Our point of difference from approaches that are based on these conceptualizations is grounded in the presumption that 'interpretation' of experiences is situated at the heart of empathy. Since interpretation and the restoration of meaning are the work of hermeneutics, we believe that a method shaped by hermeneutic insights offers a potentially valuable way forward.

Empathy

Empathy has been categorized as a key component of emotional intelligence in situations where individuals are able to connect deeply with others (Hall 2008). According to Feng, Lazar, and Preece (2004), at the macro-level, empathy has an overarching social function in relation to the creation of a non-threatening and supportive social environment. Interpretation also enables individuals to respond to stimulus, alarm, or opportunity without personally experiencing it (Jabbi, Swart, and Keysers 2007). It is this mechanism that supports fundamental behaviours within the social world (Preston and de Waal 2002).

Anderson and Keltner (2002) argue that empathic skills, relating to the interpretation of others' intentions and motivations, lead to the building and sustainability of social bonds. Empathy provides the motivation for an individual to address the needs of others in the social group in which the individual is interacting. As Preston and de Waal (2002) point out, empathy assists in the development of bonds of affiliation and affection that, in turn, support long-term social commitment. However, the development of empathy within a social group may not be driven by an implicit need to enhance the functioning of the overall group; it may be targeted towards the success of individuals within that group (Anderson and Keltner 2002; Jabbi, Swart, and Keysers 2007). Within any social group, then, opportunities exist for social enhancement, and an empathic interpretation of others may provide a key advantage for self-promotion within the social setting.

At the micro-level, empathy facilitates the capacity to understand the thoughts and feelings of others and to predict the behaviours, intentions, and motivations of others (Heite 2005; Rogers and Freiberg 1994; Stueber 2006). In educational settings, when empathic interaction of individuals occurs, an effective community of learners becomes possible. Empathy allows the teacher and the students to interpret others during dialogic engagement. Several authors (Anderson and Keltner 2002; De Vignemont and Singer 2006; Park and Bonk 2007) argue that without empathic interpretation of others the modulation of language or speech would be near impossible to manage. Subtle cues, such as body language and body movements, provided visually, offer students the knowledge of when to 'step in' and when to 'step out' within the ritual of conversational turn-taking. When these cues are focused solely on the sense of hearing, for example, a pause in the conversation or an inflection in the voice, as occurs in the on-line learning environment, the opportunity for interpretive accuracy is compromised.

Distance education and empathy

Distance education, as an educational delivery mechanism, has become increasingly prevalent, accepted, and important within the education sector. According to Moore and Anderson (2003), it has been the most significant development in education in the last quarter of a century. Providing an increasing number of people with a wider range of educational opportunities (Richardson and Swan 2003), distance education is not restricted to face-to-face interaction, nor is it restricted to occurring at the same time, or at the same place as teaching (Brown and Duguid 2000).

Technological advancements in ICTs and the development of the internet have stimulated the development of collaboration tools that have reshaped the learner–teacher relationship (Dron 2007; Peters 2003). On-line communication tools such as email, chat-rooms, blogs, wikis, and bulletin boards have been associated with a range of positive outcomes including high levels of responsive interaction between communicators, high learner satisfaction, personalization of experience, intimacy, dialogic interaction, immediacy of feedback, supported interaction, flexibility, and user-friendliness (Richardson and Swan 2003).

Empathy is central to knowledge development. Without empathic abilities or limited abilities of social actors to empathize, new meanings become difficult to construct. In the literature, the frameworks of transactional distance, social presence, and cognitive distance have, as noted earlier, been put forward to conceptualize empathic engagements. However, in these theorizations a consideration of empathy as a social relational mechanism crucial to the development of understanding has often been overlooked.

Framing up the study: philosophical hermeneutics

Hermeneutics is both a philosophical tradition and a methodological resource. The epistemological basis is derived from the phenomenology of experience as grounding for understanding how people experience and make sense of the world. In our project, undertaken as a doctoral study by the second author (Duncan 2011), we wanted to understand the meanings that teachers and students make of empathy within their com-puter-mediated teaching and learning experiences. However, Gadamer (1975, 2001) and others tell us that since meanings are never within full grasp, interpretation is necessarily required. Interpretation of text (in the wider sense) is the cornerstone of her-meneutics, as it has evolved from Kant and Hegel, to Dilthey (1961), Ricoeur (1981), and Gadamer (1975). It is also at the heart of qualitative methodologies (see Freeman 2011). Since our interest was in the interpretation of empathy by students, teachers, and researchers, rather than in the explanation or prediction of empathetic experiences, her-meneutics suited our needs.

Hermeneutics, in this study, is informed by the work of Gadamer (1975, 2001), whose interpretation of lived experience offers simultaneously a framework and a methodology for understanding empathy within an on-line environment. As a frame-work for the design of the study, Gadamer's 'moderate' hermeneutics (see Eryaman 2006) supported the overriding objective to understand the human phenomenon of empathy and students' and teachers' experiences of this phenomenon. Specifically, the aim was to interpret classroom environments devoid of face-to-face interactions and to provide rich insights of the ways in which people are able to perceive how others *feel* in such environments. The insights offered in the analyses were intended to offer interpretations of those experiences via 'text', as grasped through the language of SMC participants. Hermeneutic analyses, like these, typically provide a medium for testing and contesting theory or for developing and extending theory.

The hermeneutic focus on understanding people in the world is premised on a number of key assumptions: that (1) understanding and interpretation are part of the total human experience of the world; (2) meanings evolve and are always in process; (3) a participant's story of lived experience is filtered by his or her cultural and social location and history; (4) there will always be gaps, partial truths, and power differentials in talking about those experiences; and (5) that the present influences the story of the past. The hermeneutically inspired researcher, bringing his own virtual presence and history to the narrative, seeks to unpack and interpret the partici-pant's explicit and implicit meanings from the story presented and understand it in the same way as does the participant. In Ricoeur's words, in endeavouring to elucidate and illuminate the intended meanings of the participant, there is a 'care or concern for the object and a wish to describe and not to reduce it' (28).

The hermeneutic circle is a lens for meaning making. As a fundamental principle within the hermeneutic perspective, the circle emphasizes a part-to-a-whole process by which understanding is developed. Understandings are in constant movement between partial and whole and cannot be interpreted without reference to the context in which they are constructed (Byrne-Armstrong, Higgs, and Horsfall 1991). The whole, then, in any setting, increasingly becomes an illuminative context into which parts become easier to integrate as new information becomes accessible (Cohen, Kahn, and Steeves 2000).

In our study, understandings of empathy are presented by participants through their narratives. As participants engage with the concept of empathy, and as their pre-conceptions of empathy engage with other participants' interpretations and with the researcher's questions about empathetic experiences, new understandings emerge. The emergence of those understandings is always within an interdependent relation-ship. For the individual, understanding always requires looking 'beyond what is close at hand – not in order to look away from it but to see it better, within a larger whole and in truer proportion' (Gadamer 1975, 304).

Methodologically, then, hermeneutics offers a resource for the collection and analysis of our data. It lends itself to particular research methods and a researcher stance that is in sympathy with those methods. The stance gives recognition to the negotiation, to (virtual) presence and physicality, and to the crafting of personal relationships within the research encounter and, hence, within meaning making. Far from being bracketed out during the practical, intellectual, and social processes of a research project, relationships and experiences are constitutive elements in and hence integral to the hermeneutic circle.

The specific characteristics of the researcher in our study relate to careful listening, knowledge of the language of the computer-mediated culture, a belief in and a respect for the participants' authorship and authority of their own experiences of empathy, and a willingness to understand from the participant's perspective. The research demands an acknowledgement that interpretation of another's meanings is inherently relational. It requires a fidelity to the participant's evaluations, consistently in the analysis through the inevitable reordering, reshaping, and re-interpretation of their multi-layered narratives.

The project of hermeneutics is mirrored in the interviewing process and can be mapped in this way: the researcher develops an understanding from his own pre-conceptions and from individual explanations based on participant interpretation of their own lived experiences. The researcher understandings are then presented and exposed to alternative discourses or resistance from participants through further interviewing. New understandings emerge and these are subsequently presented to participants. Successive cycles of interpretation and re-interpretation are built into the research design to provide participants with the opportunity to evolve and develop new explanations from the interpretations of others (Herda 1999; Stapleton 1994).

In hermeneutic terms, our interpretations of the participants' meanings – both those that are foregrounded and those that are backgrounded – were expected to evolve from a fusion of horizons through the interview process. That is to say, the interview offered a means of grasping the researcher's evolving meanings of the participants' interpretations of the experience of empathy in computer-mediated environments.

Backgrounding the study: participants and environments

We chose to explore empathy understandings within similar SMC settings within two distinct on-line classes. Our decisions concerning selection of on-line participants were based around a number of key criteria: that the on-line teacher was experienced in on-line teaching; that the students were in their final year of schooling and were pursuing an academic pathway; and that the class was experienced in using Adobe© Connect™ as their conferencing medium. Our purposeful selection of participants (see Denzin and Lincoln 2000) was consistent with the principles underlying our hermeneutic framework. The two classes, both consisting of one teacher and a number of students, constituted cases for our study. Although we limited the number of cases to two (because of the logistical constraints of conducting multiple interviews), we were confident that the two classes would provide us with access to a breadth and richness of data sources for the analysis. Any generalizations, we were aware, would apply to a theoretical proposition and not to a population.

Participants were enrolled in senior secondary schools located throughout New Zealand. They had been enrolled into on-line classes by a centralized office within the Ministry of Education principally because their schools were not able to offer the students the curriculum course of their choice. Case Study 1 participants were studying New Zealand History and consisted of four female students, two male students, and the teacher (total: seven participants). Case Study 2 participants were studying Art History and consisted of three female students, four male students, and the teacher (total: eight participants).

Participants from both case studies used Adobe software in their classes for all visual, desktop sharing, annotation, and text chat capabilities. The configuration of the Adobe web presence was predominantly set up with several 'windows' or pods serving different purposes. On most occasions, students had joint access rights to pods to enable status indication, text chatting both to the class generally and other participants privately, shared annotation over PowerPoint, maps, paintings and other digital content, on-line quiz, file sharing, and whiteboard interaction. Teleconference calls were used for the audio component of the conferencing because of technical challenges encountered from individual machine configurations.

The conduct of the on-line lessons was similar for both classes with the beginning of the class usually taken up with a greeting as each participant entered the on-line virtual classroom. The initial lesson phase was often extended as additional time was frequently required in order to resolve the technical difficulties associated with participants' logging on. Typically, the objective for the day was then outlined and this was followed by questioning from the teacher to establish student progress. The content of the lesson was almost always supported through the discussion and interaction with a visual PowerPoint, maps, printed text, paintings, or with photographs. Sharing of on-line websites was also utilized. During this interaction students were given editing and interaction rights to annotate over paintings and diagrams to make points, change their status indicators, or send text messages to the group, the teacher, or other participants privately. Since there was limited capability within both classes for the use of webcam there was almost no video interaction undertaken during the two courses.

Methods informed by hermeneutics

Data collection

Interviews were the principal data-gathering tool we used to answer our research question: In what ways do SMC participants in the senior secondary school sector experience empathy? The interviews used the same Adobe Connect® conferencing software and parallel audio conference teleconference technology and techniques as were used by students in their on-line classes. The technology also allowed the researcher to connect with participants via-internet capable computers over wide geographical regions.

The research involved four distinct periods of data collection. Figure 1 summarizes the overall data collection procedure, coding strategy, sequencing, timing, and duration of phases within the research.

The participants in both case studies, separately and collectively, engaged in repeated interviews with the researcher. Whereas Phase 1 of the data collection involved an initial one-on-one interview (Phase 1a) followed by a focus group interview (Phase 1b), Phase 2 focus group interviews (Phase 2a) were conducted *before* the one-on-one interview (Phase 2b). This strategy was adopted to facilitate the collective discussion of the themes emerging from Phase 1, prior to final

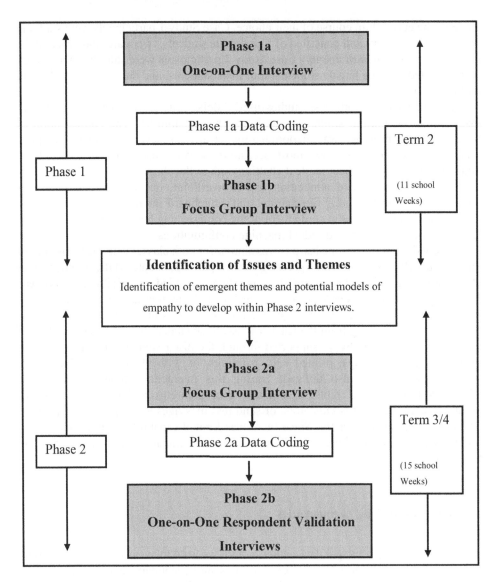

Figure 1.   Overall data-gathering approach.

independent respondent validation of the findings in Phase 2b (Hancock and Algozzine 2006).

The interviews generated data both from an individual viewpoint and a collective group perspective and allowed for alternative perspectives of the same phenomenon of empathy. These complementary interview methods provided a greater breadth and depth of data than the use of a single approach. The one-on-one/focus group, and then focus group/one-on-one strategy strengthened the credibility, dependability, and confirmability of the data through re-engagement of ideas both individually and collectively. The iterative, dialogical, and linked data collection strategy also provided the opportunity for triangulation of the qualitative interpretations within the later NVivo® data coding (Denzin and Lincoln 2003).

A total of 36 interviews were conducted over the course of the research. Eighteen interviews were completed within Phase 1 and 18 in Phase 2. Phases 1a and 2b both consisted of 15 one-on-one interviews and Phases 1b and 2a both consisted of three focus group interviews (in total 6 focus groups interviews). Given the constraints of school schedules and students' after-school commitments, eight of the 15 students were available to participate in the two focus group interviews conducted for their case study group. Eleven students were involved in at least one of the focus group interviews. The teachers participated in two focus groups interviews. Participants were, therefore, able in varying degrees to engage in the iterative data collection process. Interview schedules were converted to PowerPoint and uploaded into the Adobe on-line environment and shared both digitally and verbally with participants as the interviews proceeded. Respondents also had access to status indicators and the text chat environment, and, during the final interview, were able to use the whiteboard capability.

Both the one-on-one and focus group interviews were semi-structured to allow participants to narrate their experiences without being constricted to specific response categories. The use of pre-existing semi-structured questions also facilitated a comparison across student responses (Fontana and Frey 2003). Both kinds of interviews typically involved a five minute on-line pre-interview familiarization meeting and a routine technology check provided an additional opportunity to establish rapport with participants. All the interviews took between 30 and 40 minutes.

Importantly, in acknowledgement of the hermeneutic principle of interpretive presuppositions, the researcher's own history and familiarity and experience with on-line learning and teaching are important in the analysis. To grasp those presuppositions, data were gathered from the researcher's diary and coded as part of the data-gathering process. The diary notes, written before and during the data-gathering phases, became a valuable resource as they enabled the researcher to reconstruct participants' experiences in context without relying simply on the audio recording. The notes recorded the observations of the researcher, personal reflections on the research process, and contextual information relevant to the interview and research. Employing a hermeneutic alertness, the researcher was able to reflect critically on the meanings of the situations, rather than accepting pre-conceptions at face value. Reflections became a form of disclosure and contained insights related to the research that influenced its direction. They were used as a prompt for discussion and as an important means for seeking, from the participants at each stage in the data collection, an assessment of the alignment between participants' understandings and the ideas and observations that the researcher had noted in the diary.

Overall, the dependability of the results was enhanced through a number of strategies including: (i) the use of an iterative dialogical interview research strategy; (ii) the triangulation of participant groups, participant types (teacher/student), and interview method data; (iii) the prolonged engagement with the participants and phenomenon; (iv) the use of mutually supportive and converging data collection methods; (v) the comparison of results from the interview transcriptions for similarities of language and description across participants and methods; (vi) the opportunity for multiple constructions of understandings reducing systematic bias; (vii) the feedback from respondents in the last one-on-one interview respondent validation interview; and (viii) the auditable records.

The initial one-on-one interview

The initial one-on-one interviews were undertaken to enable the interviewer to interact personally with participants, gaining their trust and confidence (see Gillham 2000) so as to create a supportive context for them to share their understandings of empathy within on-line learning contexts. As an experienced user of SMC, the researcher was able to gain access to the participants' world and thoughts relatively easily. His personal pre-suppositions and the key themes presented within the academic literature, had, at this early stage of the research, provided him, in hermeneutic terms, with 'the range of vision that include[d] everything that [could] be seen from [his] particular vantage point' (Gadamer 1975, 301). Using his particular vantage point, he began the interview with a number of cue questions. These centred on the following factors: 'encourage-ment', 'helping behaviours', 'compassion', 'the spontaneous spread of emotion', 'tech-nical problems', 'stress and workload', 'a supportive environment', 'a strengthening bond', 'an ability to predict the behaviour or attitude of others', 'a sense of belonging', and 'cues that help in language modulation'.

In remaining open to the experiences of the participants, the researcher held his own knowledge of empathy at bay. He opened himself to the participants in what Gadamer refers to as 'true dialogue' (302), acknowledging that his own interpretation of empathy, as gleaned from the literature and personal pre-conceptions, might not coincide with theirs. He accepted their views as valid and, moreover, he believed that their views would demonstrate important experiential knowledge.

The focus groups

Two focus group interviews took place in sequential order following the initial individ-ual interviews. Established to provide a collective perspective that would supplement, refine, or extend the first one-on-one interview material, the focus group interviews offered participants a wider range of views and greater thinking time than could be offered within the one-on-one interviews. Since the teachers were also involved as SMC participants through their teaching, the hermeneutic interest in being attentive to the knowledge and voice of the other, and in accepting that 'some things . . . are against the one who seeks to understand' (Risser 1997, 15), deemed it important to incorporate, additionally, the teachers' views. Thus, separate focus groups for the stu-dents and the teachers were established. To that end, participants were brought together into three separate focus groups consisting of, in turn, the two case study student groups, and a group comprising the two teachers, the latter of which was created to acknowledge and elicit the teachers' views on SMC participation.

Through their engagement within the focus group interviews, participants were pro-vided with the opportunity to explore the meanings of their own experience with others (Ajjawi and Higgs 2007). It was hoped that during the time when an individual partici-pant was responding to questions, other participants were able to listen, reflect, and think about similar or alternative discourses thus building their understandings within the interview. However, during the first student focus group interviews students appeared more reluctant to share the depth and detail of experiences than they had in the one-on-one interviews. In comparison, the two teachers appeared comfortable sharing their ideas and did not appear to be concerned about potential negative reactions their responses might generate from the other teacher.

The researcher drew on the data emanating from the participants' discussions within the initial one-on-one interviews and his diary entries to generate material for discussion within the first focus group interview (Phase 1b interviews). As a result a number of themes that had taken prominence in the initial one-on-one interview were subsumed within other themes and a number of new themes emerged. The specific prompts for discussion within the first focus group interview centred around the following themes: 'experiencing compassion', 'experiencing encouragement', and 'experiencing helping behaviours' and 'technical problems stress and workload' within the on-line environment. These themes probed 'how participants experience a supportive environment', 'the bond or relationship between participants', 'the ability to predict the behaviours and/or attitudes of others', 'a sense of belonging to a group or on-line community', and 'cues used in language modulation'. The discussion also canvassed ideas relating to non-verbal expression including facial expression, gestures and actions and emotion.

In particular, participants discussed the theme 'cues used in language modulation' and non-verbal expression in the following way:

Kathryn: [T] I will either throw out a question or I will write up a question on the whiteboard [referring to the online whiteboard] ... the way I usually do it is I will prompt.

Joshua: ... a pause in speech or the mention of my name.

Jimmy: When there is a pause, everyone else is completely silent. They are doing their work, or the teacher is just moving on to the next slide, or finding something else.

Harold: They have this thing like when the teacher is talking you don't talk. They also have these things on the side of the classroom website where if you have a question you can click, 'I am leaving the room' or 'I have a question' or 'I don't understand', 'could you talk slower or clearer' it helps out the session.

Rita: ... sometimes we don't know exactly who she is talking to, so everyone is silent ... That is really difficult because you don't know when to communicate unless she pinpoints you right out. Like 'Rita, answer this question'.

Sally: ... you sit there and you want to ask something but the teacher is still talking and you think 'when do I ask, when do I ask?' without cutting her off.

Kathryn (T): It is just the listening to the tone and understanding where they are at with the information as well.

From the overall Phase 1 data collection (including both the initial one-on-one interviews and the first focus group interview) a number of new categories were identified. Each of the thematic categories comprised a collection of ideas and understandings shared by respondents that were found be related. As before, if new understandings did not match existing categories they prompted the creation of a new thematic category, and if an earlier category was discussed minimally, it was either merged with another or deleted. At the completion of this coding process, the following 12 thematic categories were developed: 'creation of virtual participants'; 'effect on me and others'; 'emergent disclosure of empathy'; 'empathic accuracy'; 'effect of interaction'; 'effect on learning'; 'motivation'; 'pedagogy'; 'senses'; 'effect of the interview or study'; 'comparisons of empathy'; and 'time'.

For example, in probing the theme 'comparisons of empathy'; the researcher recorded the following points made by participants:

June: ... the boys will do their 'shutting off in the corner act' and only speak when they are spoken to.

Rita: Occasionally you will get a guy who will put his two cents in, but a lot of the time the guys don't do it as much as the girls.

Jimmy: ... the girls seem as they are a bit more, 'perky', whereas the boys are the type to sit in the back and keep quiet about what they are thinking. There is your normal sort of social groups within an online classroom. The boys are your ones who keep to themselves and the girls are out there and doing their own thing.

Harold: Girls seem to be more interactive, whereas the boys, if they get asked a question they will answer it, but if not, they will like just kind of sit back and wait for the answer to be given, that's how they understand.

Joshua: I think you feel a little bit more distant in the conferencing class rather than a normal classroom. You feel a little more connected in a normal classroom with the teacher and the other students.

Mary (T): I don't think it is as intense as an actual classroom.

Jack: I think that when a question is asked in the classroom it is far easier to wait for someone to say something because there is not that direct question. Online, if someone is asking you a direct question you are more inclined to answer. It is a lot easier to hide [referring to a face-to-face classroom].

Harold: There's a lot less social time [referring to SMC]. ... You are keeping yourself focused more than if you have friends next to you in a classroom. You start socialising and getting out of work [referring to face to face classrooms]. In these online sessions you are able to stay on work.

Sally: It's not like in a normal classroom where you can talk to the other people and stuff. Because you sort of have to listen harder, so you can hear what everyone else is saying. In a normal class you would be able to talk to other people and still pick up on what the teacher is saying, if you know what I mean.

Jessica: Interpreting the teacher is quite similar, but interpreting classmates is a bit different. We don't talk about social things like I do with Mrs Smith [referring to face-to-face classroom].

The researcher then used this set of data resulting from the participants' discussions within Phase 1 (first one-on-one interview and first focus group interview) to generate questions for discussion within a further the focus group interview (Phase 2a interviews). In using this approach the researcher was giving expression to the hermeneutic principle that the discovery of truth does not involve inductive methods, but rather, that truth is in constant movement, and, in relation to this study, that participants' views of empathy in relation to on-line learning may well change over the course of time.

Whilst both focus group Phases provided a venue for group interaction, the second focus group, it was anticipated, would contribute to enhanced participant familiarity and, thus, a richer discussion of empathy in on-line environments. That is to say, it was expected that the second focus group interviews, more than the first focus group interview, would support or question the 'range of vision [presented] that includes everything that can be seen' (Gadamer 1975, 301) from a participant's perspective. For the researcher, the second focus group provided a forum for the presentation of preliminary meanings of empathy within on-line learning, as identified by the 12 categories, and offered the means to probe beyond his understanding of empathy within on-line environments. The discussion and questioning within the second focus group interview allowed for an expansion and refutation of meaning and provided an opportunity for the resolution of any ambiguity.

Thus, the second focus group interviews helped the researcher clarify his own understandings of participants' responses. In Gadamer's (1975) words, the interviewer 'opens himself to the other, truly accepts the other's point of view as valid, and transposes himself into the other's situation' (302). In the true sense of hermeneutic dialogue, the researcher casts aside any privileged status as 'one who knows'. He chooses not to be anchored to his 'vantage point', welcoming, instead, the uncertainty of knowing, and, importantly, the possibility of seeing 'beyond what is close at hand' (302). In hermeneutic dialogue, for the researcher new possibilities become open that allow him to merge his knowledge with the knowledge of the participant. The focus group interviews in the research were thus considered as opportunities for the fusion of horizons, leading to genuine understanding on the researcher's part, of the participants' responses.

Final one-on-one interview

Phase 2b concluded the data collection with the second round of one-on-one interviews. The primary objective of these final interviews was to interrogate the themes that had emerged within the second focus group interviews. Representing the final individual respondent validation point, the interview facilitated the participants' confirmation, refutation, and expansion of the researcher's interpretation of the themes that had emerged from the previous three interviews. At the same time, it provided participants with the opportunity to refine their personal understandings of empathy without the power dynamics associated with other participants.

In order to consolidate his understanding of what empathy is like in on-line learning environments, at a particular moment in history, the researcher carried out the final interviews with individual participants, placing himself in the participants' situation, acknowledging, in Gadamer's (1975) words, the otherness of the other. That is not to suggest that he did not put his view forward. Rather, it is to suggest that he endeavoured to be involved, attentive, and open. Indeed, a hermeneutic attention to the horizon of the other pervaded his entire data collection approach. It forced him to take seriously any claims or dissenting views advanced by the participants. As Risser (1997) has put it, in this kind of approach, 'one does not overlook the claim of the other, whereby one must accept some things that are against the one who seeks to understand' (15).

In hermeneutic terms, the hope was that the interviews might occasion a 'colliding event of understanding' in which the researcher's assumptions were brought to the surface. The awareness on the part of his own assumptions about empathy in on-line learning settings, brought 'with it an openness to new possibilities that is the precondition of genuine understanding' (Linge 1977/2008, xxi). From the fusing of horizons, the researcher was able to merge the data into three broad themes. Figure 2 illustrates this process for the duration of the study.

The resulting broad themes, namely, the participant, the physical environment, and the social environment, as well as the numerous sub-themes pertaining to each, represented the researcher's understanding of participants' views in relation to what empathy is like in on-line learning environments, at a specific period of time and at particular localities.

Themes emerging from the literature	Themes emerging from the first individual interviews	Themes emerging from the first focus group interviews	Themes emerging from the second focus group interviews	Themes confirmed by the second individual interviews
encouragement	experiencing encouragement	pedagogy	the participant	the participant
		effect on me and others		
		effect of interaction		
		effect on learning		
an ability to predict the behaviour or attitude of others	an ability to predict the behaviour or attitude of others	emergent disclosure of empathy		
		comparisons of empathy		
		empathic accuracy		
a strengthening bond	the bond or relationship between participants	creation of virtual participants	the social environment	the social environment
a sense of belonging	a sense of belonging to a group or online community			
cues that help in language modulation	cues used in language modulation	senses		
the spontaneous spread of emotion	non-verbal expression, facial expression, gestures, actions and emotions			
technical problems stress and workload	technical problems stress and workload	time	the physical environment	the physical environment
		motivation		
		effect of the interview or study		

Figure 2.   The development of meaning making over time between researcher and participants.

Conclusion

The methodological stance taken in this paper was founded on the hermeneutic emphasis on meaning making. The objective has been to show how a hermeneutic approach enhances an understanding of empathy in SMC. The process employed initiated a cycle of understanding. Our aim was to demonstrate how the principles of hermeneutics provide a defence of a method that allowed us to remain faithful to participants' evaluations of empathy in on-line environments. As Gadamer (1975) himself writes, understanding is not about understanding better through scientific methods; it 'is enough to say that we understand in a *different* way, *if we understand at all*' (emphases in original, 296). Against approaches that arbitrarily impose the researcher's meaning from a position of privileged authoritative knowledge, our approach instantiates the view that understanding is not a predetermined outcome. The very uncertainty of understanding is the source of its generative power to create new meanings that move closer to the participants' intent.

A hermeneutic sensibility to data collection demands greater researcher time. It forces the researcher to continuously make adjustments to his interpretation of participants' understandings – both the whole story told in terms of its details and the details in terms of the whole story (Gadamer 1975, 2001). Both the researcher's and the participants' understandings, in hermeneutic terms, are in constant movement between partial and whole and could not be interpreted without reference to the context in which they were constructed (Byrne-Armstrong, Higgs, and Horsfall 1991). In this project, the understandings of the phenomenon of empathy that evolved were informed by a hermeneutic principle of circular development of understanding. In particular, the iterative data- collection process enabled the construction, reconstruction, and negotiation of understandings, during each sub-phase interview, between the interviews, and throughout the duration of the data-gathering process. In collecting data iteratively in this way the researcher was, in Linge's (1977/2008) terms, attempting to 'bridge the gap between the familiar world in which [he stood] and the strange meaning that resist[ed] assimilation into the horizons of [his] world' (xii). The process resulted in a consensus or what Linge has named as 'genuine understanding' (xxi). Those understandings are, of course, in hermeneutic tradition, always evolving (see Freeman 2011).

A hermeneutic approach to methods is about understanding the *other* through a dialogue that allows a fusion of horizons. The collision between a participant's understanding and that researcher's interpretation of that understanding is the culminating event that 'brings with it an openness to new possibilities' (Linge 1977, xxi). This is the point where new understandings might emerge. Unearthing those new understandings has enabled a contribution to the knowledge of empathy within SMC. It has also, we propose, enabled another view of methodological practice in qualitative inquiry.

I know, that you know, that I know, that you know. (Rifkin 2009, 135)

References

Ajjawi, R., and J. Higgs. 2007. "Using Hermeneutic Phenomenology to Investigate how Experienced Practitioners Learn to Communicate Clinical Reasoning." *The Qualitative Report* 12 (4): 612–638.

Anderson, T., and D. Keltner. 2002. "The Role of Empathy in the Formation and Maintenance of Social Bonds." *Behavioral and Brain Sciences* 25 (1): 21–22.

Brown, J. S., and P. Duguid. 2000. *The Social Life of Information*. Boston, MA: Harvard Business School Press.

Byrne-Armstrong, H., J. Higgs, and D. Horsfall. 1991. *Critical Moments in Qualitative Research*. Oxford: Butterworth Heinemann.

Cohen, M. Z., D. L. Kahn, and R. H. Steeves. 2000. *Hermeneutic Phenomenological Research*. Thousand Oaks, CA: Sage.

Cohen, M. D., and D. A. Levinthal. 1990. "Absorptive Capacity: A New Perspective on Learning Innovation." *Administrative Science Quarterly* 35 (1): 128–152.

Denzin, N. K., and Y. S. Lincoln. 2000. "Introduction: The Discipline and Practice of Qualitative Research." In *Handbook of Qualitative Research*, edited by N. K. Denzin and Y. S. Lincoln, 2nd ed, 1–29. Thousand Oaks, CA: Sage.

Denzin, N. K., and Y. S. Lincoln, eds. 2003. *Collecting and Interpreting Qualitative Materials*. Thousand Oaks, CA: Sage.

De Vignemont, F., and T. Singer. 2006. "The Empathic Brain: How When and Why?" *Trends in Cognitive Sciences* 10 (10): 435–441.

Dilthey, W. 1961. *Thoughts on History and Society*. London: Allen and Unwin.

Dron, J. 2007. *Control and Constraint in E-learning: Choosing when to Choose*. London: Idea.

Duncan, W. 2011. "Understanding the Nature and Function of Empathy in Synchronous Multimedia Conferencing." Unpublished doctoral thesis, Massey University, New Zealand.

Eryaman, M. Y. 2006. "Traveling Beyond Dangerous Private and Universal Discourses: Radioactivity of Radical Hermeneutics and Objectivism in Educational Research." *Qualitative Inquiry* 12 (6): 1198–1219.

Feng, J., J. Lazar, and J. Preece. 2004. "Empathy and Online Interpersonal Trust: A Fragile Relationship." *Behaviour and Information Technology* 23 (2): 97–106.

Finkelstein, J. 2006. *Learning in Real Time: Synchronous Teaching and Learning Online*. San Francisco, CA: Jossey-Bass.

Fontana, A., and J. H. Frey. 2003. "The Interview: From Structured Questions to Negotiated Text." In *Collecting and Interpreting Qualitative Materials*, edited by N. K. Denzin and Y. S. Lincoln, 2nd ed, 61–106. Thousand Oaks, CA: Sage.

Freeman, M. 2011. "Validity in Dialogic Encounters with Hermeneutic Truths." *Qualitative Inquiry* 17 (6): 543–551.

Gadamer, H. G. 1975. *Truth and Method*. London: Sheed and Ward.

Gadamer, H. G. 2001. *The Beginning of Knowledge*. New York: Continuum.

Gillham, B. 2000. *The Research Interview*. London: Continuum.

Hall, C. 2008. "The Place of Empathy in Social Constructionist Approaches to Online Tutor Training in Higher Education." *Malaysian Journal of Distance Education* 10 (2): 33–50.

Hancock, D. R., and B. Algozzine. 2006. *Doing Case Study Research*. New York: Teachers College Press.

Heite, R. 2005. "Learning Through Love." In *Best Classroom Management Practices for Reaching All Learners*, edited by R. Stone, 51–53. Thousand Oaks, CA: Corwin Press.

Herda, E. A. 1999. *Research Conversations and Narrative: A Critical Hermeneutic Orientation in Participatory Inquiry*. London: Praeger.

Holmberg, B. 2003. "A Theory of Distance Education Based on Empathy." In *Handbook of Distance Education*, edited by M. G. Moore and W. G. Anderson, 79–86. Mahwah, NJ: Lawrence Erlbaum Associates.

Hughes, M., M. S. Ventura, and M. Dando. 2007. "Assessing Social Presence in Online Discussion Groups: A Replication Study." *Innovations in Education and Teaching International* 44 (1): 17–29.

Ickes, W. 1997. *Empathic Accuracy*. New York: The Guilford Press.

Jabbi, M., M. Swart, and C. Keysers. 2007. "Empathy for Positive and Negative Emotions in the Gustatory Cortex." *Neuroimage* 34 (4): 1744–1753.

Jolliffe, D., and D. P. Farrington. 2004. "Empathy and Offending: A Systematic Review and Meta-analysis." *Aggression and Violent Behaviour* 9 (5): 441–476.

Kehrwald, B. A. 2008. "Understanding Social Presence in Text-based Online Learning Environments." *Distance Education* 29 (1): 89–106.

Linge, D., ed. 1977/2008. *Hans-Georg Gadamer: Philosophical Hermeneutics*. Berkeley, CA: University of California Press.

Mehrabian, A. 2009. *The Balanced Emotional Empathy Test (BEES) and Optional Software*. http://www.kaaj.com/psych/scales/emp.html

Moore, M. G., and W. G. Anderson. 2003. "Introduction." In *Handbook of Distance Education*, edited by M. G. Moore and W. G. Anderson, 1–20. Mahwah, NJ: Lawrence Erlbaum Associates.

Nooteboom, B. 2008. "Cognitive Distance in and between Communities of Practice and Firms: Where do Exploitation and Exploration Take Place and How are They Connected." In

Community Economic Creativity and Organisation, edited by A. Amin and J. Roberts, 184–203. Oxford: Oxford University Press.

Park, Y. J., and C. J. Bonk. 2007. "Synchronous Learning Experiences: Distance and Residential Learners' Perspectives in a Blended Graduate Course." *Journal of Interactive Online Learning* 6 (3): 245–264.

Peters, O. 2003. "Learning with New Media in Distance Education." In *Handbook of Distance Education*, edited by M. G. Moore and W. G. Anderson, 87–112. Mahwah, NJ: Lawrence Erlbaum Associates.

Pivec, M. 2007. *The Future of Learning: Affective and Emotional Aspects of Human Computer Interaction. Game Based and Innovative Learning Approaches*. Amsterdam: ISO Press.

Preece, J. 2005. "Empathy Online." *Virtual Reality* 4 (1): 74–84.

Preston, S., and F. de Waal. 2002. "Empathy: It's Ultimate and Proximate Bases." *Behavioral and Brain Sciences* 25 (1): 1–72.

Richardson, J. C., and K. Swan. 2003. "Examining Social Presence in Online Courses in Relation to Students' Perceived Learning and Satisfaction." *JALN* 7 (1): 68–88.

Ricoeur, P. 1981. *Hermeneutics and the Human Sciences*. Translated and edited by J. B. Thompson. Cambridge: Cambridge University Press.

Rifkin, J. 2009. *The Empathic Civilization*. New York: Penguin.

Risser, J. 1997. *Hermeneutics and the Voice of the Other: Re-reading Gadamer's Philosophical Hermeneutics*. New York: State University of New York Press.

Rogers, C. R., and H. J. Freiber. 1994. *Freedom to Learn*. 3rd ed. Columbus, OH: Merrill.

Schulkin, J. 2004. *Bodily Sensibility: Intelligent Action*. New York: Oxford University Press.

Stapleton, T. J., ed. 1994. *The Question of Hermeneutics: Essays in Honour of Joseph J. Kockelmans*. Boston, MA: Kluwer Academic.

Stueber, K. R. 2006. *Rediscovering Empathy: Agency Folk Psychology and the Human Sciences*. Cambridge, MA: MIT Press.

Thompson, E. 2007. *Mind in Life: Biology Phenomenology and the Sciences of Mind*. Cambridge: Belknap Press.

Vonderwell, S., and T. Franklin. 2002. "Use of Asynchronous and Synchronous Conferencing Tools: Implications for Teacher Practice." In *Proceedings of Society for Information Technology and Teacher Education International Conference 2002*, edited by D. Willis, J. Price, and N. Davis, 155–159. Chesapeake, VA: AACE.

Advancing ethics frameworks and scenario-based learning to support educational research into mobile learning

Trish Andrews[a], Laurel Evelyn Dyson[b] and Jocelyn Wishart[c]

[a]Teaching and Educational Development Institute, University of Queensland, Brisbane, Australia; [b]Technology Education Design and Development Research Lab, University of Technology, Sydney, Australia; [c]Graduate School of Education, University of Bristol, Bristol, UK

The ubiquity of mobile devices and their use for collecting and sharing data require a reconsideration of approaches taken to managing ethical concerns in the educational research context. In the mobile age, the concept of educational research extends beyond traditional understandings and contexts due to: the wide range of mobile learning research settings, the immediacy with which mobile devices connect to social media, heightened privacy concerns and uncertainty about informed consent. This paper explores some of the ethical challenges and proposes that ethics frameworks and scenario-based learning can be powerful tools to assist educational researchers to better understand the ethical complexities of research using mobile devices and social media. An ethics framework for mobile learning research and several exemplar scenarios created during two workshops are presented. The authors make a case for this approach to be used for professional development for mobile learning researchers which may include teachers researching their own mobile learning practice.

Introduction

The growing ubiquity of mobile devices and wireless networks along with the increasing adoption of social media in higher education (Gikas and Grant 2013) and schools (Luckin et al. 2009) requires a reconsideration of ethics in the context of research in educational settings (Vallor 2012; Zimmer 2010). Our evolving networked world, with access to limitless amounts of data in a variety of media, is being increasingly integrated into everyday teaching, learning and research activities (Evans 2011). These interwoven technologies now enable educational researchers to collect data via Internet access, computer and mobile device logs, and to undertake research activities that are blurring the lines around ethical behaviours (Zimmer 2010). Many of the mobile devices currently available to students are highly sophisticated tools that include a range of recording capabilities, various social media apps, sensors for location data and wireless networking capabilities (ACMA 2013). These digital innovations are changing how we think about opportunities for learning (Traxler and Bridges 2004) and subsequently, how we think about and undertake research into learning (Vallor 2012).

This paper explores some of the ethical issues surrounding research into students' use of mobile devices and social media in educational settings. It proposes that ethics frameworks and scenario-based learning approaches can be powerful tools to assist educational researchers to better understand the ethical complexities of young people's use of mobile devices in their learning. Such frameworks and approaches are well recognized for their ability to enable professionals to build their understandings of the complexities of behaviour in a range of work and learning environments. The paper makes a case for these strategies to be used for professional development for educational researchers. In addition, we recognize the role of teachers engaged in further professional development as researchers of their own educational practice and believe that the approach proposed can be useful as they increasingly seek to investigate mobile learning as a way to provide a wider range of educational opportunities for their students.

Researching mobile and social media in educational contexts

As Sharples, Taylor, and Vavoula (2007) point out, the essence of mobile learning is the assumption that learners are moving between contexts thus making researching in mobile learning contexts 'complex and dynamic' (Traxler and Bridges 2004, 204). Research in this environment can take many forms as educational researchers including teachers researching their own practice use data collected on students' mobile devices in a wide variety of settings, including the classroom, the field, during workplace training, informal learning and students' personal study time. Pachler (2010) notes that the researcher of mobile learning is thus often working in, and across, private and semi-public domains which is a very different approach to the traditional formality of the classroom with its accepted power relations. This poses

> entirely new challenges in relation to research ethics. How, for example, can informed consent be gained in such a situation? The practices are also personal, intimately bound up with the individuals concerned as well as the formation and reformation of their identity and their relationship with members of their peer group. (Pachler 2010, 10)

In contexts, outside the classroom there are considerable challenges to researchers monitoring students' use of their mobile devices: these include possible loss of privacy, data interception and lowered control over student behaviour (Gayeski 2002; Lonsdale, Baber, and Sharples 2004). Moreover, in real-world settings how can we take bystanders' rights into account, given that 'principled sensitivity to the rights of others' is at the heart of ethics, including research ethics? (Dearnley and Walker 2010, 268) Data relating to bystanders may inadvertently be captured during students' learning activities in the field. This creates a potential ethical minefield for researchers (Vallor 2012; Zimmer 2010) in which existing ethical safeguards do not hold up (Traxler and Bridges 2004). Traxler and Bridges (2004) note in particular the difficulty for the mobile learning researcher of gaining informed consent from all parties potentially involved via a participant's Internet-connected mobile device. Additionally, mobile learning systems may not preserve persistent learner identities across sessions or across devices thus confusing the source of consent and the data to which it relates.

Social media sites, accessed by students on their mobile devices to support learning, themselves can be rich sources of data (Zimmer 2010) for varied research activities.

While this provides extensive possibilities and opportunities it also creates many occasions for privacy and ethical breaches, often inadvertently. As Gardner (2014) points out, the understandings relating to identity and privacy have changed with the emergence of the digital era. Furthermore, following their experiences in Mobilearn, a pan-European mobile learning project, Kukulska-Hulme et al. (2009) highlight other issues such as who owns the products of this, often conversational, learning (online or phone discussions and interactions with websites and blogs). In a similar vein, McAndrew, Godwin, and Santos (2010) note practical difficulties of posts to public blogs being protected from research activities and the need for users to accept the public nature of any posts they make. Added to this, the increasingly globalized nature of the world and consequent interactions with different cultures heighten the complexity of understanding the concept of ethical research (Keatinge 2010) when researching the learning opportunities associated with mobile technologies and social media.

The design of the mobile devices themselves is an obvious contributor to these concerns. Highly portable, they are an ideal tool to support learning across contexts, creating the challenges highlighted above. Furthermore, the multiple functions of mobile phones and tablets, particularly their use for taking photographs and videos and the ease with which these images can be uploaded to file-sharing and social media websites, create huge risks of privacy infringements (Wishart and Green 2010). Furthermore, the much smaller size of mobile devices compared to traditional cameras and video cameras makes them 'infinitely more portable and unobtrusive', allowing surreptitious recording to be much more likely than was possible with the older technology (Aubusson, Schuck, and Burden 2009, 243). Again, because of their size, theft and loss of mobile phones are quite common, thus compromising data security (Wishart 2009). Furthermore, mobile devices are not just physical tools, they are also gateways to cyberspace and virtual worlds. This has been a long-standing issue for the mobile learning research community, with researchers finding their goal of identifying how educators can capitalize on the potential of emerging technologies to enhance teaching and learning regularly blocked by lecturers' and teachers' concerns about what their students can access.

Zimmer (2010) suggests that the increasing integration of the Internet and of web 2.0 environments in research is creating not just challenges in relation to research in the digital era, but also conceptual gaps. As well as notions about what constitutes consent, these gaps include understandings around privacy and effective strategies for anonymizing data, and the inexperience of ethics committees in relation to research in these new environments (Zimmer 2010). An illustration of these conceptual gaps is highlighted by Zimmer's discussion of a research project involving Facebook and the failure of the researchers to keep their data anonymous despite applying the usual strategies for de-identifying data. Other concerns associated with researching in mobile and social media environments in a connected world relate to cyber safety and the difficulties of controlling these environments from a research perspective (Traxler and Bridges 2004). As Vallor (2012) suggests, educational research in digital environments requires different ways of thinking.

Scenarios and ethics frameworks

Scenarios, or simulated case studies, are a means of articulating issues from real-world experiences and exploring ways forward for the future (Kamtsiou et al. 2007). They are often used in teaching ethical issues for such an approach supports contextualization, exploration of multiple perspectives, reflection and opportunities to develop collaborative solutions (Herrington, Oliver, and Reeves 2003). Ethical scenarios themselves are usually complex and not clear-cut, presenting the varied viewpoints and conflicting priorities of the stakeholders, thus avoiding glib solutions (Spinello 2003). The aim is not to teach people right from wrong but to equip them with the ability to reason about ethics. They represent a participant-centred learning process since those working through them are actively engaged in finding a solution. Scenarios have the advantage of making ethical issues concrete, moving 'from abstractions to realities' (Costanzo and Handelsman 1998). Their embedding within a specific context assists professionals prepare for the ethical challenges they will face in their own practice.

For researchers exploring mobile learning and social media, scenarios can provide a way of considering the complexities of dynamic and unpredictable mobile learning situations and develop a personal ethical response. However, in order to provide a foundation for such ethical development we must first consider the need for a relevant framework on which to base the discussion and analysis of the scenarios.

In educational research today, as Hammersley and Traianou (2012) point out, research ethics framing tends to be prescriptive, and the expectation is that researchers are informed by their experience of their relevant educational association's codes of conduct; examples include the British and the American Educational Research Associations' guidelines. Additionally, if the researchers are working with teachers of young people and children then this expectation would include the teachers' 'Duty of Care' statements as outlined in their relevant national teaching standards. However, mobile learning researchers have noted that this can lead to a multiplicity of 'rules' that are dutifully reviewed in the initial stages of research project design but are then liable to be overtaken within the project's lifetime as students adopt new technological practices (Wishart 2009). Additionally Davies (2013) notes, when reflecting on ethical challenges involving research into pervasive computing, how first gaining appropriate ethics approval is a significant challenge in itself. He goes on to make the point that questions of how to adopt an ethical approach to pervasive computing extends beyond the research domain, affecting practitioners as well. This, too, is relevant to the field of mobile learning research where it is teaching colleagues who are often key actors. Batchelor et al. (2012) go so far as to describe this as 'innovative teachers being ensnared within the everyday prosaic, unstructured and utopian perspective' of mobile learning. In this space they believe there is an onslaught of technologies bringing with it a range of ethical concerns. More simply Clark et al. (2009) use the term 'digital dissonance' to describe the teachers' tension with respect to learners' appropriation of Web 2.0 technologies in formal educational contexts. However, Batchelor and Botha (2009) propose that a move from a rules-based system of addressing ethical concerns in mobile learning to a value-based system could accommodate new technology developments. This could be helpful for all mobile learning researchers, including teachers researching their own practice.

Indeed a simpler, value-based way forward is to adopt the approach introduced thousands of years ago by the Greek philosophers and accepted in medical practice (Beauchamp and Childress 1983) with its four widely accepted ethical principles: do good, avoid harm, autonomy and justice. The first two of these are fairly self-explanatory. The principle of autonomy requires that people have the right to be treated as autonomous agents, with their own self-directed goals and rights to choice, self-determination, privacy and control over personal information. Persons with diminished autonomy, for example, students, must have their autonomy protected by responsible others (Howard, Lothen-Kline, and Boekeloo 2004). We can consider the principle of justice as implying equity of access to mobile learning opportunities and to the mobile devices as tools to support learning.

This approach was used to develop the framework shown in Figure 1 during an early discussion workshop held in the UK for mobile learning researchers investigating potential teaching and learning applications for personal digital assistants, the then most commonly available mobile device in education, and reported by Wishart (2009). The matrix shown arises from the combination of the four accepted ethical principles as described above with what were deemed, at the discussion workshops, to be the key, most pressing ethical concerns that teachers and other educators come across in their everyday work. It was believed that these would also be of high priority in research into mobile learning.

Each cell in the table, where a key ethical concern intersects with an underpinning ethical principle, becomes an opportunity for reflection as to what is current practice and what is good practice. Not all intersections will give rise to relevant concerns, depending on the situation under consideration, and in some instances it will be hard to balance principles. For example, with researching the use of mobile devices to capture and share images, 'avoid harm' may conflict with the concept of 'respect user choice' embodied in the more general principle of 'autonomy'. Indeed what constitutes doing good, avoiding harm, autonomy or justice can itself be controversial and is likely to vary across situations and cultures. However, the act of considering the range of ethical concerns involved will alert the researchers to the need to come to an agreement with the students and teachers participating in the research with respect to that key concern.

The framework should be used as a starter to generate initial discussion about ethical issues and then form the base for the production of scenarios to use to practice debate and generate the skills of ethical analysis. It can then be employed by researchers

	Do Good	Avoid Harm	Autonomy	Justice / Equal Access
Personal information				
Images				
Informed consent				
Ownership				
Data storage and protection				
User-generated content				

Figure 1. Original ethics framework for mobile learning research.

in analysing the specific challenges of the situations that arise in their own research into mobile learning. The following section describes how such ethical discussions developed at two international workshops, and we share some of the results of the workshops in the form of the scenarios produced.

Methodology

The aim was, therefore, to devise exemplar scenarios to support mobile learning researchers and teachers engaged in researching their practice with mobile learning. The approach taken followed a participatory design methodology (Spinuzzi 2005) and involved having experienced researchers collaboratively design scenarios, having first discussed and agreed the underpinning ethics framework to be used.

The scenarios to be presented in this paper are derived from those which were developed by participants at two further discussion workshops dealing with ethics and mobile learning held in 2012. The first workshop took place at the *mLearn 2012* conference in Helsinki, which attracted researchers and practitioners from around the world. The second was conducted in Sydney as the focus of the annual Mobile Learning Research Workshop, conducted by *anzMLearn* (the Australian and New Zealand Mobile Learning Group) with attendees from Australasia. As described above, the scenarios grew out of key ethical concerns surrounding mobile learning research raised by participants at the two events.

Each workshop began by examining the principles and frameworks that inform the codes of conduct and policies which guide technology use in educational institutions generally. The limitations of classic rules-based (deontological) approaches were noted by participants and the need for a more flexible method, one more akin to that deployed in a situation ethics approach which prioritizes flexible guidelines allowing each situation to be addressed as a unique case, was identified. This new approach, though, would need to enable researchers to deal appropriately with ethical issues arising in the shifting contexts and changing situations that characterize mobile learning. In open discussion, participants brainstormed their own concerns about teaching with and researching mobile learning and from this list the ethical issues felt to be most important were prioritized for scenario development.

From the key concerns put forward at the two workshops for scenario development, the following related to ethical issues surround mobile learning research:

- Boundaries such as those between formal–informal, public–private, home–school, real–virtual and so on. Mobile devices are 'boundary objects' (Pimmer and Gröhbiel 2013) easily carried between contexts enabling information more usually restricted to one context to be accessed in another.
- Privacy – as boundaries are crossed, there are opportunities for researchers observing students' use of mobile devices to infringe privacy. With differing cultural perspectives on privacy, managing the risks can be a challenge. There is also the need to obtain permissions by third parties, for example, on work placements, and the possibility of accidental inclusion of outsiders in student-generated content.
- Anonymity versus respecting the desire to self-publish. This is a particular challenge where the accepted practice of ensuring that participants in a research

project remain anonymous conflicts with students' desire to celebrate their work via the social media apps on their mobile phones.

- Ownership of data – whose data are on the mobile device or on the server and who owns it. This is a particular concern in respect of ownership of images where perception varies along with the context where the images were captured, at college or in a park, for example.
- Participants' awareness of device capabilities such as what data are being logged by the different apps and who can view it.
- Accessibility – people who are differently able and/or less educated or who may come from different cultures, and what this means regarding both the range of mobile devices available to the proposed participants and costs, for example, for devices to access the Internet and usage charges incurred.
- Risk analysis – the unexpected consequences of complexity, boundary crossing and changing circumstances as a research project set-up in one space is impacted by information and sociocultural expectations from others.

Cross-tabulating these with the four key ethical principles introduced above resulted in the new framework shown in the next section. This section also presents several exemplar scenarios for educational research derived from this framework. These are selected from the wider range of scenarios developed at the two workshops and their use in the professional development of mobile learning researchers will be discussed.

Outcomes

The new matrix created through further discussion with a wider range of international researchers at the two workshops described above to form an ethics framework for scenario generation is shown in Figure 2.

The scenarios generated were found to provide tools to support professional development, for example, in the area of introducing new researchers to educational research into mobile learning. The scenarios generated at the Helsinki workshop are now hosted online by the International Association of Mobile Learning (http://www.iamlearn.org) for that very purpose. By enabling participating researchers to focus discussion on ethical issues, it was found that the realistic scenarios generated could assist them to work through potential issues and develop strategies to deal with and, if possible, avoid ethical breaches before they happen.

Examples of the scenarios generated at the two workshops are given below.

Scenario 1: Whose story is it?

Key issues highlighted

Maintaining anonymity versus respecting a participant's desire to keep up a digital identity.

Research question

How can learners be protected as producers of student-generated online content?

	Do Good	Avoid Harm	Autonomy	Justice / Equal Access
Boundaries				
Privacy				
Anonymity				
Accessibility				
Ownership				
Awareness				
Risk analysis				

Figure 2. Resultant framework outlining potential ethical concerns in mobile learning research.

Description

It is common to see people on the spot when a major event happens using their mobile phones to upload images and comments to the Web, whether to formal news sites or via social networking sites such as Twitter. Sometimes these citizen journalists are anonymous through the use of pseudonyms, while sometimes the profile associated with their comments provides full details of their name, job and location.

Belinda and Asif are teacher trainees who are interested in researching learning opportunities offered by citizen journalism. Could it effectively boost children's literacy? They intend to get the students to create an online newspaper using handheld mobile devices with cameras to capture stories and then upload them to the school website, where anyone can view the content. However, there are various issues that are concerning the class teacher.

Questions to be considered

- To what extent should anonymity be enforced? What is the students' opinion as to whether their anonymity should be protected by the school? How could Belinda and Asif lead a discussion with the students to make them aware of the potential risks versus the benefits of having their work identified by their family and friends? Who else should be asked: parents, school principal?
- How will the issue of inclusion of images or recordings of interviewees or bystanders be dealt with? Is this an ethical or legal issue, or both? Should third parties captured in multimedia files be asked for their consent to stories being written about them and the posting of these to the school website?

- How can the researchers ensure the students respect other's privacy in an age where capturing of content is easy and ubiquitous?
- Will the online presence of the newspaper be publicized? How can the student journalists be protected from cyberbullying if anonymous posts are allowed about the news items via social media linked to the school website?

Other similar situations

Researching students engaged in Nature study may mean discussing whether a participant's discovery such as an invasive species, a visiting migrant bird or the location of a rare breed should be anonymized or publicized. In this case, there are the possible consequences for the species itself as well as the learners to be considered.

Scenario 2: Who pays?

Key issues highlighted

Equity of mobile learning research based on the bring your own device (BYOD) model and involving learners who come potentially from varying economic backgrounds.

Research question

How can mobile learning research using the BYOD approach be made equitable for all student participants?

Description

A research student Otto is planning his Ph.D. on developing learning activities bridging inside and outside school contexts for teenagers using mobile phones. The learning will be focused on field trips or visits, such as those to museums and art galleries. He expects them to text or post online from the location of interest. His access to research funds to support his research is very limited and he therefore intends to ask the students to use their own mobile devices.

Questions to be considered

- Should Otto provide devices to students who do not have them? If some students do not own a phone, is their learning enhanced by the activity in any way? How can economically disadvantaged students be taken into account? Will the research throw light on these equity issues? How will the type of research, for example, whether it is voluntary or not, and the requirements for what the devices need to do affect Otto's response to these questions?
- How will the learners be connected? What implications will this have for usage charges incurred by the students? If using up their text allowance on a school project, does that impact on their social life and the ability to text their friends? What about unintended costs associated with exceeding data limits, for example, sending multimedia files such as photos or video? How aware are the learners of different connectivity routes and their associated cost such as 3G (internet connections) versus Wi-Fi? If choosing Wi-Fi,

will there be a loss of immediacy if the learners need to go to a hotspot to upload their data?

- What types of devices are available within the participant group and how will this impact on the design of the learning activities? Will Otto or the school be able to support the teenagers if they have technical problems in using their devices for the activities?
- How will parents feel about the research? Will there be pressure on them to ensure their children can access learning by providing them with mobile phones of the required functionality, displacing education costs from school to parent? Also, what about the parents' support for the learning activity: will they consider the use of mobile phones at school work?
- If there are instructions, information or templates that needs to be downloaded by the students to their devices to support them whilst on location there may well be a cost to the researcher of putting these into a suitable, universally accessible form, such as EPub.

Other issues that may arise

Research into students engaging in off-task activities using their own mobile phones.

Other similar situations

Similar issues of equity will apply for any research which relies on access to a service or technology paid for by the learners, or where participants may, through different abilities or needs, be more or less able to access the service or use the technology.

Scenario 3: Where do you stop?

Key issues highlighted

Boundaries such as those between formal–informal, public–private, home–school, real–virtual and so on.

Research question

How should mobile learning researchers engage with any of their participants' extended social networks when investigating how learners use social media to support their formal learning?

Description

This is a project funded by a National Teaching Innovation Grant and run by John, a university lecturer who is concerned that his topic is perceived by students to be a particularly 'dry' one. He is interested in developing his teaching to make more use of collaborative learning opportunities enabled by students using mobile phones to access social networking sites at a time and place convenient to them. He has set a task to be completed on line through, say, Facebook, where students work with each other on a set task.

Questions to be considered

- Who should be asked for consent and how should they be informed? The research participants and their 'friends' who will see the activity online or just the participants? What about friends of friends? How to raise awareness amongst the participants' friends of the research?
- When is a discussion 'on task' and thereby included and when is it 'off-task'? Even a discussion centred on a set task may contain personal information and references to outside events or people. However, is that not so much a contamination of the data but important data in itself?
- Becoming a member of the community? What are the pros and cons of having John as a 'friend'? What is he to do on coming across unexpectedly personal information?
- How to anonymize the data?

Other issues that may arise

The now common use of pseudonyms and temporary email addresses online – how does a researcher identify the actors in this situation and ensure their consent?

Other similar situations

Any research involving a mobile device that is used in personal as well as work contexts is likely to lead to access, wittingly or unwittingly, to personal information unrelated to the project. A participant may be unaware when giving consent to the research of the extent of the personal data stored on the phone.

Scenario 4: Whose data is it anyway?

Key issues highlighted

Conflicting responsibilities towards patients in the face of new technologies: either to maintain confidentiality of patient data by keeping to tried-and-true methods of record keeping, or to research the introduction of mobile technology to collect and transmit patient data and the training of medical staff to undertake this appropriately.

Research question

How can teaching hospitals, health science educators and researchers protect patients' privacy while investigating the introduction of new mobile and wireless technologies for biomedical data collection by trainee medical staff?

Description

Increasingly mobile devices and wireless networks are being used by nurses and doctors to collect patients' biomedical data. Patients in teaching hospitals traditionally sign a consent form that they agree to trainees treating them under supervision, but are they aware of the increased risks associated with data transmission on wireless networks, and are the trainees also aware of the risks and how to avoid them?

Miranda is a trainee nurse on a work placement to a large metropolitan teaching hospital. She is being shown how to collect vital medical data from the patients in her care using an experimental program which runs from a smartphone. The training that her nurse educator and the mobile technology researchers give her focuses on the functionality of the program and how to successfully upload patient data to a cloud-based database of patient records. Some of the patients are aware that a new procedure is being tested, but are mostly too sick or too elderly to fully understand what is going on and the privacy implications. Miranda has to give a class presentation about her placement once she returns to university and would like to keep some of the data she has gathered for that purpose.

Questions to be considered

- How can the nurse educators and mobile researchers raise Miranda's awareness of the risks of data interception, her moral and legal rights and responsibilities regarding the health information, and who owns it and what can be done with it?
- Are the consent forms signed by the patients inclusive of the new data handling procedures? If not, is it legal to collect their data? How could patients be made aware of the potential risks to their privacy so that they can give genuinely informed consent? Do patients have the right to say 'no'?
- What are the boundaries to how the information can be used? Can Miranda present it to her fellow students? Can she keep the data for use in a final-year research project that she has to complete before graduation, or for future reference to support her life-long learning?
- Does it make a difference if it is *her* smartphone that is being used during her work placement? How would this impact on the researchers' access to data collected on her phone in order to evaluate potential breaches of patients' privacy?
- Would the situation be any different ethically or legally for participating nurses and doctors who are employed by the hospital as trained permanent staff?

Other similar situations

Any research into work-based training where trainees can potentially photograph or record data belonging to the organization or record situations that occur in the organization using their smartphones or tablets/iPads.

Discussion and conclusions

The combination of being tasked to develop the final framework shown in Figure 2 and the scenarios derived from it which formed the outcome of the workshops demonstrate the wide-ranging and complex nature of the ethical issues that face those engaged in mobile learning and social media research. At times ethical and legal issues were hard to separate, for example, when does persistent photography of an individual come under the legal definition of harassment? As digital tools progressively play a role in people's private lives and in learning activities, the line between personal and pedagogic uses of these technologies is becoming more and more blurred and ethical concerns like these cannot be ignored. All too often the media, as well as the literature, are full of stories of unethical behaviour and inappropriate use of mobile phones

(Campbell 2006; Ling and Donner 2009). In an effort to minimize harm, many schools have completely banned them. However, as Dyson et al. (2013) point out, this is putting our students at a serious disadvantage. We must face the fact that they:

> now live in a mobile world, and their working lives will be part of that world: no better place to start equipping them to deal with the mobile technology challenges that they will encounter through life than to acknowledge that our educational institutions belong to that world too. (Dyson et al. 2013, 411)

By exploring mobile technology-based teaching and learning activities, such as mobile-supported fieldwork, work placements and complex project work using multimedia content created or captured with mobile devices, teachers and educational researchers are promoting the means for students to become life-long learners well beyond their formal years of education. This extends opportunities for educational research way beyond traditional boundaries, into the home, into cyberspace and into unforeseen futures.

Therefore, this study has proposed scenario development combined with an active discussion of an ongoing ethics framework as a way to ethical professional development of educational researchers and teachers as researchers of their mobile teaching practice. Scenario generation was found to be an effective method of stimulating discussion and raising awareness of potential ethical concerns, with the experience of workshop participants ranging from doctoral students to tenured professors. In particular, first engaging the participants in discussion and planning the underpinning ethics framework to be used enabled both participants' voices to be heard and the subsequent discussions tailored to their needs and interests. Thus we conclude that collaboratively creating scenarios and ethics frameworks can provide a way of understanding the issues associated with research centred on mobile learning and its potential consequences, and a means to develop appropriate solutions.

In addition, these scenarios provide a resource that researchers can work through to explore the issues of concern to them and possible solutions to resolve these issues. We recommend, above all, finding a path to develop 'personal responsibility' and address the hard issues in ways that promote good practice in the use of mobile technology and social media for research in teaching and learning contexts.

Disclosure statement

No potential conflict of interest was reported by the author(s).

References

ACMA (Australian Communications and Media Authority). 2013. "Privacy and Personal Data." *Emerging Issues in Media and Communications*. Occasional paper 4.

Aubusson, P., S. Schuck, and K. Burden. 2009. "Mobile Learning for Teacher Professional Learning: Benefits, Obstacles and Issues." *ALT-J Research in Learning and Teaching* 17 (3): 233–247.

Batchelor, J., and A. Botha. 2009. "Liberating Learning." Paper presented at the Educational Association of South Africa, Amanzimtoti, South Africa.

Batchelor, J., M. Herselman, J. Traxler, and W. Fraser. 2012. "Emerging Technologies, Innovative Teachers and Moral Cohesion." In *IST-Africa 2012 Conference Proceedings*, edited by P. and M. Cunningham. Dublin: International Information Management Corporation.

Beauchamp, T. L., and J. F. Childress. 1983. *Principles of Biomedical Ethics*. Oxford: Oxford University Press.

Campbell, S. W. 2006. "Perceptions of Mobile Phones in College Classrooms: Ringing, Cheating, and Classroom Policies." *Communication Education* 55 (3): 280–294.

Clark, W., K. Logan, R. Luckin, A. Mee, and M. Oliver. 2009. "Beyond Web 2.0: Mapping the Technology Landscapes of Young Learners." *Journal of Computer Assisted Learning* 25 (1): 56–69.

Costanzo, M., and M. M. Handelsman. 1998. "Teaching Aspiring Professors to be Ethical Teachers: Doing Justice to the Case Study Method." *Teaching of Psychology* 25 (2): 97–102.

Davies, N. 2013. "Ethics in Pervasive Computing Research." *IEEE Pervasive Computing* 12 (3): 2–4.

Dearnley, C., and S. Walker. 2010. "Mobile Enabled Research." In *Researching Mobile Learning: Frameworks, Tools and Research Designs*, edited by G. Vavoula, N. Pachler, and A. Kukulska-Hulme, 259–276. Oxford: Peter Lang.

Dyson, L. E., T. Andrews, R. Smyth, and R. Wallace. 2013. "Towards A Holistic Framework for Ethical Mobile Learning." In *The Routledge Handbook of Mobile Learning*, edited by Z. Berg and L. Muilenberg, 405–416. New York and London: Routledge.

Evans, B. 2011. "The Ubiquity of Mobile Devices in Universities – Usage and Expectations." *Serila* 24 (3): S11–S16.

Gardner, H. 2014. "Reframing Ethics in a Digital World, A Few Moments with Howard Gardner." DML Research Hub. Accessed December 3, 2014. http://dmlhub.net/ newsroom/expert-interviews/reframing-ethics-digital-world.

Gayeski, D. 2002. *Learning Unplugged: Using Mobile Technologies for Organizational Training and Performance Improvement*. New York: AMACOM.

Gikas, J., and M. M. Grant. 2013. "Mobile Computing Devices in Higher Educations; Students Perspectives on Learning with Cellphones, Smartphones and Social Media." *Internet and Higher Education* 19: 18–26.

Hammersley, M., and A. Traianou. 2012. *Ethics in Qualitative Research: Controversies and Contexts*. London: Sage.

Herrington, J., R. Oliver, and T. Reeves. 2003. "Patterns of Engagement in Authentic Online Learning Environments." *Australian Journal of Educational Technology* 19 (1): 59–71.

Howard, D. E., C. Lothen-Kline, and B. O. Boekeloo. 2004. "Using the Case-study Methodology to Teach Ethics to Public Health Students." *Health Promotion Practice* 5: 151–159.

Kamtsiou, V., T. Koskinen, A. Naeve, D. Pappa, and L. Stergioulas. 2007. "A Glimpse at the Future of Technology Enhanced-professional Learning: Trends, Scenarios and Visions." In *European Networking and Learning for the Future. The EuroPACE Approach*, edited by A. Boonen and W. Van Petegem, 293–313. Heverlee: EuroPACE ivzw-Garant Publishers.

Keatinge, D. 2010. "Ethical Dilemmas and Cultural Considerations in using Action Research and Participatory Action Research." Paper presented at 8th ALARA World Congress Participatory Action Research, Melbourne, Australia.

Kukulska-Hulme, A., M. Sharples, M. Milrad, I. Arnedillo-Sanchez, and G. Vavoula. 2009. "Innovation in Mobile Learning: A European Perspective." *International Journal of Mobile and Blended Learning* 1 (1): 13–35.

Ling, R., and J. Donner. 2009. *Mobile Communication*. Cambridge: Polity Press.

Lonsdale, P., C. Baber, and M. Sharples. 2004. "A Context Awareness Architecture for Facilitating Mobile Learning." In *Learning with Mobile Devices: Research and Development*, edited by J. Attewell and C. Savill-Smith, 79–85. London: Learning and Skills Development Agency.

Luckin, R., W. Clark, K. Logan, R. Graber, M. Oliver, and A. Mee. 2009. "Do Web 2.0 Tools Really Open the Door to Learning: Practices, Perceptions and Profiles of 11–16 Year old Learners." *Learning, Media and Technology* 34 (2): 87–104.

McAndrew, P., S. Godwin, and A. Santos. 2010. "Research 2.0: How Do We Know about the Users that Do Not Tell Us Anything?" In *Researching Mobile Learning: Frameworks, Tools and Research Designs*, edited by G. Vavoula, N. Pachler, and A. Kukulska-Hulme, 277–288. Oxford: Peter Lang.

Pachler, N. 2010. "Research Methods in Mobile and Informal Learning: Some Issues." In *Researching Mobile Learning: Frameworks, Tools and Research Designs*, edited by G. Vavoula, N. Pachler, and A. Kukulska-Hulme, 1–16. Oxford: Peter Lang.

Pimmer, C., and U. Gröhbiel. 2013. "The Affordances of Social Mobile Media for Boundary Crossing." Paper presented at the Swiss Society for Research in Education Conference: Integrating formal and informal learning, Lugano, August 21–23.

Sharples, M., J. Taylor, and G. Vavoula. 2007. "A Theory of Learning for the Mobile Age." In *The Sage Handbook of Elearning Research*, edited by R. Andrews and C. Haythornthwaite, 221–247. London: Sage.

Spinello, R. A. 2003. *Case Studies in Information Technology Ethics*. 2nd ed. Upper Saddle River, NJ: Prentice Hall.

Spinuzzi, C. 2005. "The Methodology of Participatory Design." *Technical Communication* 52 (2): 163–174.

Traxler, J., and N. Bridges. 2004. "Mobile Learning – The Ethical and Legal Challenges." In *Proceedings of MLearn 2004*, edited by J. Attewell and C. Savill-Smith, 203–207. London: Learning and Skills Development Agency.

Vallor, S. 2012. "Social Networking and Ethics." In *The Stanford Encyclopedia of Philosophy* (Winter 2012 Edition), edited by Edward N. Zalta. Accessed October 5, 2014. http://plato. stanford.edu/archives/win2012/entries/ethics-social-networking/

Wishart, J. 2009. "Ethical Considerations in Implementing Mobile Learning in the Workplace." *International Journal of Mobile and Blended Learning* 1 (2): 76–92.

Wishart, J., and D. Green. 2010. "Identifying Emerging Issues in Mobile Learning in Further and Higher Education: A Report to JISC." JISC. Accessed October 5, 2014. http://www. jiscdigitalmedia.ac.uk/blog/entry/resources-for-mobile-learning.

Zimmer, M. 2010. "But the Data is Already Public: On the Ethics of Research in Facebook." *Ethics and Information Technology* 12: 313–325.

Index

Note: Page numbers in **bold** type refer to figures
Page numbers in *italic* type refer to tables
Page numbers followed by 'n' refer to notes

For Product Safety Concerns and Information please contact our EU
representative GPSR@taylorandfrancis.com Taylor & Francis Verlag GmbH,
Kaufingerstraße 24, 80331 München, Germany

Printed and bound by CPI Group (UK) Ltd, Croydon, CR0 4YY
01/05/2025
01858513-0005